# What others are say



'This is an important book, good common sense stuff we forget when we are stuck in the middle of the chaos of change. It covers all you really need to know in an easy read.'

**Professor Melanie Bryant, University of Tasmania**

~~~

'You know you are doing it right, when other change managers (me) share your content with their clients and early career change resources, point to it and say: 'You see?! What she said!'. Could not be more timely Jen, a much needed resource'.

**Gilbert Kruidenier, Experienced change program and project manager**

~~~

I wish I had read this a few years ago, hands down the most sensible and valuable read on workplace change. Strips away the fluff, simplifies the complex and just gets down to business.

**Simon Hunter, GM Comms, CSIRO**

~~~

We've all heard 'change is the only constant' and in a digital world the pace of change is ever increasing. If you don't have a handle on how to deal with it, you could well be on a fast track to irrelevance. Luckily, this book is available to help you avoid that. It's a "must read" for the uninitiated to change. And a "should read" for those who want to improve how they do it.

**Dr Andrew Maher, Chief Digital Officer, Aurecon**
~~~

~~~

Dr Jen has de-mystified the field of change management and provided professionals at all levels of an organization the basic tools, knowledge and inspiration to make informed decisions about small and large scale changes in their organization. I was reminded of having the courage to "hold the space of potential in front of you", even when that space is unclear and may only come into focus as the work progresses. I usually insist on beginning with the end in mind, but in some cases we have to use the project to discover the future.

**Gabrielle Steckman, CEO, My Integra**

~~~

This is a book I wish I had written. Not only for the quality and the diversity of the content, but also for the way it was written; i.e.: 'out loud'. I admire the down-to-earth manner in which Jen approaches our field. Could you use this book as a checklist? Probably. But a fool with a checklist is still a fool. That's why this book is packed with conversations, links and references to scar tissue of people who have been there. Definitely a plus for our community and for everyone who is new to the profession.

**Luc Galoppin, Director, Reply-MC, Founder Organizational Change Practitioners LinkedIn Group**

~~~

'This is what is missing in bringing change to life – highly practical stories and conversations on the 'how'. Only an experienced practitioner who also has deep academic understanding of a broad array of disciplines could bring such clarity so quickly. I am regularly asked for a 'primer' on leading and managing change and
~~~

this is now my 'go to' recommendation. And just in case you are wondering if experienced practitioners will get anything out of it, I will share that I learn from Jennifer in every interaction we have. Jennifer's insights and experience shine through as she takes existing concepts and clarifies, extends and applies them. We can all benefit from the perspectives and the 'Conversation Starters'.

**Gail Severini, Managing Director, Symphini Change Management Inc.**

~~~

Jennifer has a unique ability to guide people towards an outcome. Her incisiveness and directness are mixed with a deep understanding of human nature and decision making. She approaches difficult conversations with both candour and compassion. You may not want to hear the truth be told but you know you need to listen. Conversations of Change is relevant to anyone who wants to manage people, drive change or understand the subtle positive influences one can make in the workplace.

**James Shirley, Project Manager, Digital Projects, AKQA**

~~~

Jennifer has an uncanny knack of getting to the heart of what matters when it comes to making change stick. Her passion for promoting conversation on this topic is infectious, this book has already triggered new and better thinking for me on my next adventure.

**Kelsey Miller, Senior Banking Executive**

~~~
~~~

# Conversations of Change

# Conversations of Change

## A guide to implementing workplace change

Dr Jen Frahm

Jennifer Frahm Collaborations Pty Ltd
Melbourne, Australia

ISBN: 978-0-6480879-9-1 (AUS paperback)



Edited by Leanne Frahm and A.T.H. Webber

# Contents

PART III. CHECKING THE PERIPHERALS

# Acknowledgements

They say it takes a village to raise a child. I'd argue the same can be said with regards to getting a book into your hands. I have been insanely blessed to have a community to support me in the development and publication of this book. To list them all would be to increase the cost of this book as I would need many, many pages. But I do need to call out a few people in particular.

First, and foremost, my very clever editor who also happens to be my mother. How lucky am I? Any errors you find in this book, will be because at the age of 47 I still sometimes don't listen to my mother.

A big call out to my virtual editorial board – Kate Ware, Melissa Dark and Susan Lambe. Your continued support, cheering, counsel, and reality checks have been invaluable.

My publishing 'buddy' Lena Ross – a well-timed coffee made all the difference. Thank you for challenging me on mindset, and huffing and puffing to 'I know I can, I know I can'.

And Steve Vallas and Sean Callanan from Chunky Media, I'd like to say a well-timed walk around the lake made a huge difference, but perhaps it was more remarkable that I could retain the counsel with heatstroke imminent. Look forward to many more laps in cooler climes.

# Foreword

In the busyness of our business lives, we are constantly bombarded with change. New competitive threats, processes, compliance obligations, technology and new opportunities place pressure on our businesses and our people to adapt. Change may be abundant and all consuming, but the expertise to manage change remains in short supply. Change is not getting less complex as we manage in a connected global economy, so a strong understanding of how to effect change well is important for leaders at all levels.

In this practical and enlightening book Dr Jennifer Frahm takes us on that journey through the elements of a successful approach to change. Dr Jen leverages her considerable expertise and depth of understanding of the practical implementation of change to map out an adventure for a manager facing any level of change complexity.

In the book, Dr Jen quotes a well-known passage of Machiavelli:

'It must be considered that there is nothing more difficult to carry out nor more doubtful of success nor more dangerous to handle than to initiate a new order of things'

What this book outlines is an antidote to the common experience that advocates of change experience. That experience is well summarized in the following passage of that Machiavelli quote:

'for the reformer has enemies in all those who profit by the old order, and only lukewarm defenders in all those who would profit by the new order; this lukewarmness arising partly from the incredulity of mankind who does not truly believe in anything new until they actually have experience of it.'

Dr Jen supplies anyone approaching change with guidance on how to avoid the usual experience. This book outlines how to organize the work of the change, how to define a compelling purpose for the change that can win better than lukewarm support and how to lead a change to effective implementation by learning from experience. Throughout the book these lessons are reinforced by Dr Jen's depth of experience and stories from her global network of change management experts and practitioners. The approaches in this book are not just theory. They are lessons worn with the sheen of experience and the odd scar of battle.

In the digital era, we have one advantage that was not available to the Change Agent of Machiavelli's time, the power to people to connect, share and solve problems in global networks. Effective and responsive organisations leverage the potential of change agents connected into communities by networks to lead, influence and execute change. The complexity, scale and speed of modern change demands autonomy and collaboration.

As the Margaret Mead quote goes

"Never doubt that a small group of thoughtful, committed citizens can change the world; indeed, it's the only thing that ever has."

With a rising focus on digital transformation around the world, this book is timely. You will need to lead a change soon, perhaps as early as tomorrow. Before you tackle your next change, take the time to learn the many lessons of this important contribution to the literature of change management.

Simon Terry

Change Agent

ChangeAgentsWorldwide

Simonterry.com

ChangeAgentsWorldwide.com

# Introduction

## A GLIMPSE OF WHAT IS POSSIBLE

'Of course, Joanne, I'm excited about the opportunity, I believe I can make quite the difference.'

Sitting at your desk now, those words are coming back to haunt you. Only six hours ago, you confidently told your manager you were certain of delivering the biggest workplace change of your career. And now you have no idea where to start. Well, that's to say, you have an idea of what needs to happen and your manager had provided some direction on that – ultimately, she wants to see a 25% reduction in operating costs. You can see some opportunities for improvement and have some good ideas on what to change. But how? How to make this change happen? What if your employees don't like it and won't make the changes? What if other managers are resentful and try to sabotage? What if the customers and suppliers become nervous of the changes? Knowing what to do is very different from knowing how to do it…

Welcome to the world of organizational change management.

So, you sit down and fire up Google. Keyword by keyword you get further confused. The results seem to contradict each other and throw up more jargon by the minute. Apparently 70% of changes fail. It appears that people's default is to resist change. There seems to be 100 different methodologies on how to implement change. How the hell do you navigate this stuff and not screw it up? Have you just accepted a career limiting 'opportunity'? You're thinking back to past experiences and can remember initiatives where there was little change management. There were signs…

The mojo was missing. Things just felt different and not so good!

People felt like they were mushrooms – kept in a dark corner and fed, umm, cow poo.

You and your colleagues didn't feel there was much information out there about what was happening so you started making up very plausible pieces of information to fill the gap. These plausible pieces of data may or may not have been true.

People were feeling more emotional than usual at work, some scared, some cynical or worried.

There was increased sick leave.

There was increased work load.

The managers were more stressed than usual.

The press was suggesting that the company was not doing so well financially.

You definitely don't want that to happen again.

Breathe. It's going to be okay. You have this book. There's a reason why it's called a guide to implementing workplace change. It's going to help you navigate through the magical, complex, jargon and buzzword laden, often obtuse and overly theoretical, world that is workplace change.

You're not alone you know. Managers are increasingly expected to initiate, lead and execute change in the workplace with little knowledge or experience of change management. And this is very difficult to do without a guide.

As you work through this book you should find it helps you work out what you need to do, who you need to help you, and what to consider in your workplace change efforts. There's an additional bonus, too. In doing so it offers you ways to build your broader team's capability to absorb, initiate and execute on change. The book is full of interviews with experienced practitioners and industry experts and conversation starters for your team.

**Part 1: Shaping up – the decisions you need to make**

Chapter 1 looks at the various change scenarios facing today's managers and matches these with the type of change expertise you might want to work with. Of course, you may not have the opportunity to bring in or work with any change expertise, so you will find that the book offers 'self-serve' as an option.

Chapter 2 provides a primer to the often confusing world of organizational change management. Baseline definitions are provided with scope, inclusions, and exclusions. You'll know what is in this book, and what is not. Chapter 2 also introduces the

Change Management Institute's *Change Maturity* framework as a way of thinking about where you are now, and what that means for your organization's change trajectory.

Chapter 3 delves into who the key characters in change management are. In understanding the difference between change agents, change leaders and change managers, you can work out the best way to use the strengths of these people.

Chapter 4 is specifically for those who can recruit a change resource either internally or externally.

Chapter 5 helps you define your vision for change and how you are going to measure success. In thinking through the barriers and the enablers of success, you can keep momentum and manage the roadblocks.

Chapter 6. Now that you know who you are going to work with and what you are working towards, you are in a better position to identify what change model or framework you want to use (if any).

**Part 2: Moving forward**

Chapter 7 picks up on change capability. You can't drive change through on willpower alone; there needs to be an uplift in change capability. This becomes particularly pertinent in organizations that seek to be agile and responsive and continuously changing. Change capability can be seen at an individual level, a team level, and an organizational level.

In working through your change, you need to think about how ready your audiences are for the change you want to bring in. Chapter 8 works through change readiness by way of definition, and considers how you measure it and use the results.

Chapter 9 addresses the dreaded topic of Change Resistance. With a simple change of perspective, change resistance evaporates and you have greater opportunities for engagement.

Chapter 10 addresses your change communication. It's a big area and some would say the most important component of workplace change. We'll navigate through elements and dilemmas about marketing, branding, internal communication, social media, dialogue, and monologue.

Change 11. Those who say change communication is not the most important component of change are probably saying it's change leadership. In Chapter 11 we dig into change leadership – matters of authenticity, control, surrender, stewardship and strength based approaches.

At this point you can probably take a moment to pause and check the peripherals, those elements that infiltrate today's organizational change domain and can clutter or confuse.

**Part 3: Checking the peripherals**

Chapter 12 gives you the opportunity to consider next practices in organizational change management and how they might benefit your work. These next practices include Future of Work agendas, and topics like WOL, Neuroscience and Agile.

In Part 2, you've worked through what is considered best practice in change management. Chapter 13 picks up on the myths and big debates of organizational change management and asks, 'Do they really matter?'. The answer is yes, but maybe not to the extent that those who write about them suggest. Regardless, you're cautioned not to throw babies out with bathwaters – there's merit in considering these debates and myths in your change program.

Chapter 14. You've got to the end of the book and feel empowered, and more change capable. You think you might like to take this new knowledge further in practice after you have this change under your wing. What's next? Chapter 14 wraps up the book by considering the next options – accreditation, further education, and communities of practice.

Chapter 15 is the cheat's chapter. Ahem, I mean the time efficient chapter. In it I summarize all of the relevant adventures. If you are feeling confident, identify your adventure and jump straight to it.

Calmer now? Read on ...

PART I

# Shaping up - the decisions you need to make

# 1 Choose your own adventure

Well hello there! Haven't you got yourself a challenge ahead of you! And isn't it a bit of a confusing world for the uninitiated? Heck, even for the initiated it can get a bit complex. The good news is it needn't be. We're going to work through what's ahead of you in bite-size pieces with lots of prompts and calls for action. I like to think of it like those 'Choose your own adventure' stories we had when we were kids (okay, assuming you are over 30, and if you're not, then google it. Was way cool!)

Not sure what I mean? Well, let me lay out four scenarios that you may be faced with. Depending on which scenario fits your circumstances, this book will offer different value for you.

Let me explain.

There are three variables to consider in your adventure:

- How well do you know what the change to be delivered is?
- How much internal resourcing do you have for change management?
- How much budget do you have to hire specialist resources?

Depending on your answers to these questions, you could have very different adventures ahead of you. Regardless, they all start with Chapter 2, as this is a baseline understanding of what you will be doing. The next chapter helps you distinguish between those who know what they're talking about, and helps you ask the right questions. Part one of this book is all about the decisions you need to make to get yourself set up for change success. Part two covers the elements that are necessary for a successful change, and Part three addresses components of change management you hear about and might want to consider.

But back to those adventures ahead of you.

In working out the best way to lead and implement the outcomes you have confidently promised your manager, you need to consider the three variables (known solution or change, resourcing, and budget).

Some of you reading will be about to embark on Adventure 1.

### ADVENTURE 1

- **You do not know what the change is to be,**
- **You have no internal change resources,**
- **You do have budget.**

You're in the position where life will get easier if you hire a change consultant to help you shape up what your change program will be, and how you approach it.

You may wish to recruit contract change resources or use internal change resources.

Part 1 helps you work out what you look for in specialist change resources (consultant, contractor or internal talent), how to evaluate their work, and what they will be expecting you to support or lead. Part 1 also helps you understand the methodologies and frameworks they will talk about or include in a proposal for you.

Part 2 helps you navigate the core components of the work they will be doing. It helps you understand what quality looks like and what you should be seeing.

Part 3 is particularly relevant if you're bringing in a consultant or a contractor as they can be more up to date with the contemporary issues of change. Sometimes they can be very invested in the big debates, and this section will help you work out what you need to pay attention to and what you can let slide.

**ADVENTURE 2**

- **You do know what the change is to be,**
- **You have no internal change resources,**
- **You do have budget.**

If you know what the change is to be, you may not benefit from bringing in a change consultant, although you might wish to use a consultancy for resourcing the execution. You do have to decide whether to bring in someone for a permanent role or external assistance. You can either recruit contract change resources or use internal change resources. Part 1 helps you navigate the recruitment and how to evaluate their work.

Part 2 helps you navigate the core components of the work they will be doing. It helps you understand what quality looks like and what you should be seeing or the kind of discussions you will be having.

Part 3 is also useful in having conversations with your change management resources on the contemporary issues of change.

There will be aspects that you may wish to include for a fresh delivery of change, as opposed to what has always been done.

## ADVENTURE 3

- **You do know what the change is to be,**
- **You have internal change resources,**
- **You do have budget.**

In what seems in the most favorable of adventures, you need to understand how your internal change resource model works, and how to end up with the right one for your initiatives. Part 1 will help you in articulating what kind of change initiative you are responsible for, which helps in the selection of your change resource. Part 2 helps you understand your change resource performance and quality. Often internal change resources are less up to speed with the latest in the literature and the big debates as their focus is on what is happening in the organization. The need to maintain currency of change knowledge is not as great for them, and they don't tend to invest much time in professional development. So, Part 2 is still important to consider in conjunction with your resources. Part 3 might give you some topics to talk about with your change resource and work through if there's value in that. The value in Part 3 is doing things differently and with more effectiveness, depending on your situation.

## ADVENTURE 4

- **You may or may not know what the change is to be,**

- **You have no internal change resources,**
- **You have no budget to hire anyone.**

Oh. Okay, so this is not really the space you want to be in, but be reassured, plenty have done it before and succeeded. Treat this book as a little Jiminy Cricket sitting on your shoulder, whispering words of encouragement and suggesting next steps. You should be able to absorb a lot of what needs to be done, and have enough of the lingo that you sound confident and can actually make change happen. It just won't be as easy as the other adventures. Read Part 1 to understand what qualities and attributes to adopt or bolster, select a change approach that resonates with you, and define your vision. Look out for the self-service conversation starter prompts. From there, use Part 2 to rally the troops and execute your change. Chapter 12 in Part 3 are important to read; they may yield some epiphanies and opportunities to fast track the benefits of your change.

So, chosen your own adventure? Let's go…

CONVERSATION OF CHANGE: LIAM HAYES, CHIEF PEOPLE OFFICER AT AURECON

**Dr. Jen**: The first question I've got for you: When was the first time you put your hand up to lead a major change? And what was that experience like?

**Liam**: So, the first time I led a major change was when I was working for one of our predecessor businesses called Connell Wagner.

It was at a time when a new CEO had taken over, as the previous CEO had retired, the organization really hadn't gone through any major change in at least 10 to 20 years, and the new CEO had a vision in terms of the future of the organization and embarked on what was really a business transformational project.

As part of that I was asked to lead the culture / change stream that worked across the other functional bodies. They were looking at everything from organizational structure to leadership to business strategy.

**Dr. Jen**: So that's in at the deep end. That's as big as a change as you're going to get to be asked to lead. In the book, one of the things I've grappled with is how to distinguish between organizational change management, and change management which is often more aligned with the project phasing. How did you perceive change? As a broader organizational change management piece? Or did you see it as more a discrete change process?

**Liam:** Yeah, it certainly was an organizational change piece. We really tried to shift the whole organization and not look at just one particular thing. Everything, systems or processes to org structure. So, it was different to the more recent change management project that you have been working with us on, which was the implementation of our new global HR system, 'Workday' which was a very discrete piece of work. Whereas I go back to the Connell Wagner project, which was a very large program of work that was set to go over multiple years, and we'd engaged IBM business consulting to actually come and help us with that change.

**Dr. Jen:** Right. So, prior to that piece of work kicking off, what had been your knowledge of organizational change?

**Liam:** Very little. Probably what I learnt at university. But really when I was at university, organizational change in HR add business degrees wasn't really a topic. So, the extent of my knowledge was really through reading books out of my own interest. But I really learned a lot in that first change program, and was lucky enough that the consultants that I worked with from IBM and other organizations really mentored me. I was just really lucky that they were experienced change professionals that had been there and done it before with larger organizations. They really took me under their wing and I got a lot out of that. I think you can read books which help in terms of learning from other people's experiences, but the problem I found with a lot of books on this topic is that they are very theoretical – I think change has to be very practical. And when you've been through an experience and come work alongside others that have done the same, your kind of learn as you go.

**Dr. Jen:** Which adventure does this belong to, if we think about what we framed up in the book?

**Liam:** I think it was Adventure 1. Everything about both that and also a more recent Workday change resembles Adventure 1. Albeit with the Connell Wagner one, we knew we wanted to shift the organization. We knew the types of things we had to do to shift the organization.

But we really didn't know what that looked like. We had an idea. But when we started it, we really had to work out what were the things we're actually going to do and then that how did that impact our staff. Likewise, with the Workday one, we knew we were implementing a new HR system. That's all we really knew and particularly because Workday use the Agile methodology in terms of implementing their system, we were really discovering what the impact of the change was going to be as we were going and design the system.

**Dr. Jen:** I guess it's interesting because in Adventure 1 you don't know what the change is per se but you've got budget and you've potentially got resources there. Also, there might still be a level of discomfort involved for the stakeholders – the fact that there is this ambiguity and uncertainty around what the final stage is. Did you find it was that way or does it become something that's more empowering and liberating because you can be more creative with it?

**Liam:** I find it more empowering and liberating because you can be more creative. I think sometimes the danger with change or transformational projects, is that if you're going with a fixed mind view in terms of what the end outcome must be, it does limit you in terms of possibly coming up with better ways of implementing the change.

Certainly, with Workday, we learned along the way. We knew the end goal was to implement one global HR system across the business. That was really our end goal. We had a budget to do that, and we had a team in place to do that. But we didn't know what the design was going to look like, and one of the things we went into that project saying was that we actually, in a lot of cases, wanted to start with a blank sheet of paper because we had processes and systems that had been in the business for a long time. We didn't want to take bad processes and put them into a new system. So, I actually think it's better starting with that mindset of, 'yes, you've got something you have to deliver it', but you should really keep an open mind on how you deliver and what that looks like. Particularly if you want to engage with wider stakeholders in the business is very important in terms of helping co-design that.

**Dr. Jen:** In terms of your experience, so you've started off with that experience quickly with IBM and the consultant, and you've had inhouse change practitioners at Aurecon. You've bought people like myself in as 'externals'. How would you categorize your experience with working with change practitioners? What's the value in it? What are the challenges? What are the frustrations? Where's their benefit?

**Liam:** My experiences have been positive and it probably goes back to my Connell Wagner example of having people that were not just interested in terms of helping us implement the change, but actually wanting to help building my capability of change. That they saw that their role would come to an end at some point but knew this change of transformation would continue. So, that was a really positive experience for me and I think it's probably helped me as well — I'd like to think that there are now good change practitioners that kind of work within the business because I know what good looks like and I can hire better.

I think there are people out there that promote themselves as change practitioners. But I do think there's a big difference between someone that may have worked once on a change project that's part of a team and someone that is a trained change professional that has worked on a number of change projects and they are the people you're really looking for. I think that's where sometimes maybe the change practitioners get a bad reputation because of people, selling themselves as change practitioners when they're really not.

**Dr. Jen:** Okay, so if you've gone out for lunch, a networking lunch, sitting next to someone who's just said that they're about to introduce a major change in their organization for the very first time, what's going to be your advice to that person?

**Liam:** Hire a specialist change person if you don't have one. Because I think too often organizations fall into the trap of looking at say: 'yes, we've got this change project and it's a project we need to deliver', then frantically look around for someone who looks like they have some spare time and just say 'let's get them to lead the change.' I think that's why we see such a high failure of change projects. It's because we don't get the right people leading it. And so, if you have a major change project, yes there is a cost. But the greater cost is failure. So, invest up front and put a change person in place. Because I think you'll see the real benefits in terms of a more successful ad hoc greater chance, the more successful outc

# 2 Through the looking glass

The title to Lewis Carroll's much praised sequel to Alice's Adventures in Wonderland, 'Through the Looking Glass and What Alice found there' often reminds me of what it is like to search 'change management or organizational change management' in Google. What a fantastical world with language as hard to understand as the Jabberwocky's poem and characters that start to resemble Tweedle-dee and Tweedle-dum. Certainly, it can be argued that workplace change resembles a great board of chess!

Even within the industry, confusion and argument abounds. Many within the change management profession struggle with how to describe what they do. If you poke into the varying change management groups on LinkedIn, periodically there are varying debates on what to 'rename' change management. And goodness gracious me, if you though 'Change Management' was jargon, you should see the alternatives being suggested *(Change Enablement, Transition & Transformation Management, Organizational Behavioral Change Facilitation).*

This chapter seeks to highlight four core points of confusion and offer some clarity to help with your progress on your adventure.

**POINT OF CONFUSION 1 The difference between Organizational Change Management and Change Management**

I see Organizational Change Management as addressing the broader organization and its change in strategy, structure, or culture. Change Management is a narrower focus – the facilitation of people through a discrete change. It raises the distinction between project change and organizational change. Most change projects have a methodology (either project or change), not all organizational changes have a dedicated methodology. Not all change managers work on organizational changes, but most organizational change managers will use change management.

There really are no absolutes with this stuff.

*Why does this matter to you?* Depending on the scale of the change you have in front of you (e.g. a discrete project, or a larger organizational change) the value in the models, frameworks, and resources differs. Some of the common change management frameworks are more suited to discrete change projects, others are suited to large organizational changes. Someone who has only ever been a change manager on discrete change projects like new system implementations may not be suited to helping you with changing the culture of your organization.

There are two 'official' change management industry bodies at the moment vying for world domination. The Association of Change Management Professionals (ACMP) and the Change Management Institute (CMI). While these may not be of direct value to you – it is useful to know about them as they are responsible for actively developing the change management profession. Both can still be considered in early development – if you look at the ratio of people who define themselves as change practitioners versus members.

CMI was founded in Australia and has grown to have chapters across NZ, Asia, Ireland, Canada, the UK, and some membership in the USA. Some of the more important artefacts of CMI are the

Change Maturity model and the Change Competency models. They have a Change Management Body of Knowledge and an accreditation process.

ACMP is founded in the US and has chapters in Europe, Middle East and North Africa, Canada, and Latin America. Similar to CMI, it has attempted to standardize the industry with the use of The Standard and accreditation. We'll talk more about accreditation and industry standards in Chapter 14. I don't think in and of themselves they are a bad thing, if they were more agreed upon and established you possibly would not be feeling as confused and lost and looking for books like this. Accreditation however does not guarantee are good practitioner.

But we are far from standardized and uniform. So here we are.

Renowned blogger and industry expert Gail Severini, notes the two bodies view change management a little differently.

The Association of Change Management Professionals (ACMP) defines change management to be the application of knowledge, skills, abilities, methodologies, processes, tools, and techniques to transition an individual or group from a current state to a desired future state, such that the desired outcomes and/or business objectives are achieved.

'Change management processes, when properly applied, ensure individuals within an organization efficiently and effectively transition through change such that the organization's goals are realized. Change management is an integral part of the overall change process and ideally begins at the onset of change'.

ACMP's definition assumes that the organization has agreed upon the need for change and has identified the nature of the change.

The Change Management Institute (CMI) hasn't taken up the challenge of definitions but offers some clues in their definition of a Change Management Practitioner in their Competency Model.

> 'A Change Management Practitioner has mastery of the change principles, processes, behaviors, and skills necessary to effectively identify, manage, initiate, and influence change, and manage and support others through it'.

CMI's definition of the change management practitioner leaves some room for the idea of emergent change. Not all organizations have agreed upon the need for change and identified the nature of the change. As we will discuss in later chapters, that can be a strategic decision – a deliberate decision to co-define and cocreate the change with the members of the organization so that there is more commitment to the change.

Further, Severini notes change management focuses narrowly on the facilitation of people from the current state to the desired state. It deals with expediting three things: understanding, commitment, and alignment, which helps people change the way they think about their roles, leave behind current mindsets and competencies, and dive into new thinking and build new capability. From this you can infer that the 'change management' has more of a focus on the people during change. Organizational change management will include the people and the structural and strategic elements.

Often you will see change management referred to in technology context – and this is often a more technical discipline, referring to the management of upgrades and releases. We're not talking about that in this book. Additionally, it is popular to eschew planned and episodic change for 'emergent change'.

My experience with emergent change is it tends to describe the process of initiating change, more so than the experience of implementing change. Emergent change models tend to talk to opportunistic innovation and creative continuous improvement. However, just because the goal of the change is emergent, it does not mean that you will not benefit from a dedicated focus on how you implement the changes coming through.

Having said all of this, there is so much lack of clarity on the difference between the two terms – organizational change and change management, it would pay you to ask the question upfront of anyone you are talking to about change management or organizational change management. Where there is opportunity in this book, I will call out if there is a distinction in the use of the term.

### POINT OF CONFUSION 2 Role clarity

The next point of confusion is often who does it – change agents, change champions, change managers and change leaders. Chapter 3 talks about the roles of change, and so I'll leave definitions of change sponsors, change agents, change managers, change champions, change communicators, and change analysts there. What you do need to know at this point is that there is a difference between the roles and the terms are often used in a less than precise fashion.

At the risk of minimizing the importance, though, of role definition; anyone can implement change or even manage change. Let's face it, we all do it on a regular basis – we change houses, physical states, move neighborhoods, deal with changing fortunes and finances. But in choosing your own change adventure you need to make sure the appropriate people are accountable for change. If you stick with 'anyone can do it', there's a fair chance nobody will do it. Role clarity provides accountability, and without accountability change can take a glacial speed.

### POINT OF CONFUSION 3 Methodologies and frameworks

Part of the world of change is the language of frameworks and methodologies. There is an old well-worn joke 'Methodologies give people with no ideas something to do'. And it's kind of true, kind of not. Having a framework to guide you or a methodology to follow can save you a lot of time, if it is fit for purpose. And this is where it gets challenging – determining fit for purpose. At the most blunt and crass level a change methodology outlines:

- How to come up with the change idea (design or architect)
- How to build you change solution and supporting collateral (build or prototyping)
- How to prepare the people who will be affected for the change (readiness)
- How to execute the change (deployment)
- How to support post change (hyper care)

- How to measure and adjust as needed
- How to make the change sustainable

This list of imperatives is required whether it is an organizational change, or a discrete project change.

All the change management methodologies and frameworks out there will address some or all of these imperatives. Within each imperative there can be a change model, or framework that informs the intent and process. They can take the form of 3 step, 4 stages, 8 steps, you name it. Think of models and frameworks like recipes – helpful to give you a sense of the process, and timing and what ingredients you need. The quality of ingredients and condition of the cooking environment does make a difference to the outcome. We'll look at these in more depth in Chapter Five.

**POINT OF CONFUSION 4 Scope of change**

The scope of workplace change is an interesting consideration and one you need to be aware of. Setting clear boundaries on what your change covers and what it doesn't is important to resourcing and budgets. But here's the rub – regardless of your scope definitions it is rare that your change occurs in isolation of others. You need to be thinking about the interdependences and interfaces. This can be an iterative conversation – in that as your change evolves and progresses you may entertain 'scope creep'. See this is the other fun thing about change – change 'changes'. Six months into your change process, things will have changed – leaders, key stakeholders, business focus, strategy and external market conditions. These can all have impact on your change scope.

In considering these four aspects of confusion and unpacking some of the definitions, it might now be time to have a conversation with your peers or team that drives some clarity in these areas.

## CONVERSATION STARTERS

**Some of the conversations you might want to have right now with those around you are:**

- To what extent is the change I wish to lead an organizational change and to what extent is it a change project?
- If it is a change project, how does it align with the broader organizational changes?
- What are our preliminary assessment of who will fill what role? Who is missing?
- Do we have a change methodology that is in use in our business?
- What do I think the scope of my change is – what does it include, what does it exclude and what is it dependent on?
- What extent can we expect the scope to change?

## IMPLICATION FOR YOUR CHOICE IN ADVENTURE

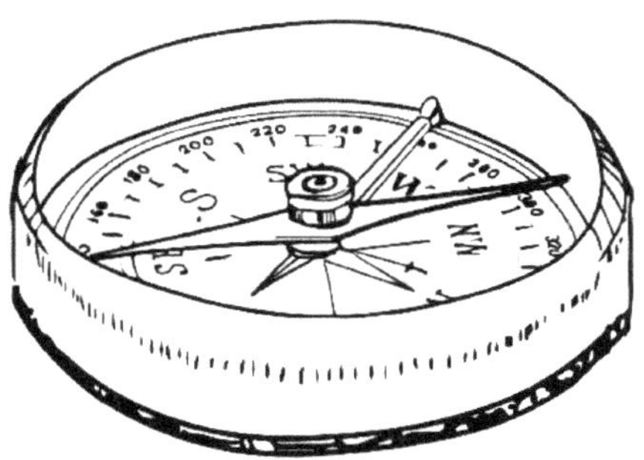

### ADVENTURE 1

- **You do not know what the change is to be,**
- **You have no internal change resources,**
- **You do have budget.**

As you will most likely to be engaging a change consultant to help you shape up what you want to do and how you will do it, this chapter should empower you to ask your change consultant some defining questions about their approach. It will also assist you in evaluating their proposals and statements of work as to their fit for purpose with your engagement.

### ADVENTURE 2

- **You do know what the change is to be,**
- **You have no internal change resources,**
- **You do have budget.**

In this instance, your immediate need is to recruit. Understanding what the common misunderstandings are will help you navigate engaging with a recruiting agencies or directly with candidates.

### ADVENTURE 3

- **You do know what the change is to be,**
- **You have internal change resources,**
- **You do have budget.**

This chapter is great for you – you can really cut to the chase with your internal resources to understand how they operate and make sense of their world. The conversation starters at the end of the chapter will be particularly useful in framing up your initial conversations with them. The time you invest in this mutual sense-making will pay big dividends!

### ADVENTURE 4

- **You may or may not know what the change is to be,**
- **You have no internal change resources,**
- **You have no budget to hire anyone.**

Meep! I'm still wincing for you. Ok, so this chapter provides you some guidance in understanding what phases of change are that you need to plan for with the blunt and crass outline of what methodologies do. Role clarity is probably a bit easier for you – for now, you are it. You are accountable and there is probably not much ambiguity about that – although you are encouraged to be thinking about who you could co-opt from your peers to form a working party that fills these roles! To that extent, it doesn't really matter how you define organizational change management. Though, I am hoping that you have got some good insights into the things you want to be thinking about with your change.

In the next chapter, we will pick up on the issue of role clarity in your change efforts. This should help you to get clear on who will play which roles and as such, who will be accountable for what you need them to do.

Note: Thoughts on associations and Point 1 in this chapter has been influenced by conversations with and blog posts of friend and colleague Gail Severini. I can't recommend her work enough and if you head to https://gailseverini.com you will find a wealth of resources on this topic.

# 3 Of change agents, change leaders and change managers

Regardless of the Adventure you are embarking on, as you sit with your laptop googling 'change management', you'll find that there are a number of people who seemed to be charged with doing things, and sometimes the names of these people are used interchangeably. This introduces a lot of confusion about who does what in change. As you start to think about the change you want to introduce, you need to think about who will be helping you in the change and what their roles are in change. This chapter names the roles and provides an understanding of what they do (or should do), and what you might want to consider as you navigate forward.

Let's start with the change leader, as in many circumstances this may actually be you!

## CHANGE LEADER

These are line managers and senior managers who are prepared to actively and vocally sponsor, support, and role model the changes you are introducing. Ideally, they should work alongside the people identified as change champions (we'll get to them) to ensure that they are supported. In many companies, change leaders end up having the key success criteria of the change project built into their performance review. They are also integral in determining consequence management of the change – for example, what happens when people work around the change.

***'Leaders take people where they want to go.***

***Great leaders take people where they don't want to go.'***

*Rosalyn Carter*

Leadership of change is not for the faint of heart. It's hard work, as often you need to hold the space of potential in front of you, while others work very hard to close it down! We'll talk more about it in Chapter 11 but ideally, change leaders are good communicators, inspire confidence and faith, and are comfortable with leading with authenticity and empathy. They are not 'spokespeople' and they do not shy away from difficult decisions.

## CHANGE SPONSOR

The change sponsor is a formal role assigned often to the head of a steering committee (known as a 'steerco'), but not always. If your organization is using a formal project methodology you will most likely have a project sponsor, and this may actually be you. The change sponsor is ultimately accountable for change, and keeps a close eye on the issues at hand and what it will take to remove barriers. A change sponsor should not be particularly involved in the day-to-day running of the change, but their attention will ramp up when things are getting tricky. A change sponsor should be seen as a support and a facilitator, not someone to please. Sometimes there is a lot of overlap between change sponsors and change leaders, but it is not uncommon to have one change sponsor and multiple change leaders in the business. The change leaders lead the people, the sponsor ensures the barriers to change are removed whether they be political, resource-led, or structural.

## CHANGE AGENT

If you've stuck your hand up to initiate, lead and execute change, there is a fair chance that you are indeed a Change Agent. The change agent is often the person who introduces and champions the new idea. Additionally, the change agent is usually responsible for taking the activity into the world of 'Business As Usual' (e.g., post change activity). Everett Rogers in his change bible *The Diffusion of Innovations* (1962) described a change agent, as 'an individual who influences client's innovation decisions in a direction deemed desirable by a change agency'. Critically, 'the change agent not only seeks to obtain the adoption of new ideas, but may also attempt to slow down diffusion and prevent the adoption of undesirable innovations'. (p. 28). Further, in contrast to the ideas above of the change agent as part of the business, Rogers saw the change agent as being different to the client (i.e., by experience, education and social system).

The issue of whether your change agents should be internal or external is a contentious one. There is an argument for external change agents – when your organization is so wound up in inertia that it is impossible for anyone to initiate and champion change, you do need to hire in an external change agent (possibly a change consultant or a new leader who knows they are coming in to drive change).

But there is equally a strong argument for making change agency a core capability in all your people in the organization.

Charles Hardman, Managing Director of 4D Solutions, provided a fascinating example of change capability building by distributed change agents in a previous organization:

*... We consciously made every employee an 'agent of change' and including 'change' as a key result area on everyone's performance reviews. Our view was that every employee was responsible for solutions. I appreciate that this isn't necessarily how it all worked in practice, but it did allow us to be very clear with our expectations; whilst providing the opportunity to every employee to make things better. i.e. employee engagement. Likewise, we had no long-term appointed change managers – rather we had people who had a 'manage change' key result area.'*

It's an interesting approach – one that would require significant change maturity within the business. We talk more about this in Chapter 7.

## CHANGE CHAMPION

Champions and agents are often used interchangeably – in my view an agent is an instigator of change, the champion is a nominated representative of the change team.

Change champions are employees who are identified as having strong influencing and communication skills and a passion for new ways of doing things. This community will be identified, recruited, inducted and provided early education and opportunity to 'play' with the technology (e.g. the 'sandpit' or environment where you can test and experiment with prototype), walk through the new processes, or be involved in workshops to define new behaviors. They should be equipped with three domains of knowledge –

project timing and activity, technical knowledge of the change (e.g., what is changing and why), and change management knowledge to encourage user adoption (how to lead, influence and coach people through change).

In some cases the change champions may be used to conduct local briefings and training. Ideally, you want geographically located champions – although with more companies becoming comfortable with Enterprise Social Networks, we are starting to see more digital or e-change champions. Working out how many change champions is determined by several pragmatic considerations:

- What do you want them to do and how much time will that take?
- How many do you need to access your target audience, especially those companies that have geographic footprints widely spread?
- The differentiation of what the business units do. For example, can one change champion attend to multiple business units or they are so different in culture and purpose the one champion would not be able to influence them?
- How are you going to induct and manage the change champion network (e.g., times for check-ins and queries)?

I must say the term 'change champion' is becoming more out of favor. It's often viewed as the kiss of death, or associated with previous initiatives where they were not used so well. In organizations where many changes are introduced concurrently, change champions can be a scarce resource – often the person in the business who is an influencer and passionate about new things is sought after by many. The solution to this is, as Charles Hardman identified earlier, to build a change capability across the whole of the organization.

## CHANGE CONSULTANT

A change consultant is usually someone who is external to the organization and who can come in to your business, perform a diagnostic phase, and produce recommendations on the way forward. They usually keep themselves to the high level activity – diagnosis, strategy, planning, and evaluation. They don't tend to do the 'doing' side of change, although many have a team associated with the consultancy who can go in and execute the change (e.g., change managers, change communicators, change analysts, training people).

You're going to want a change consultant to help you understand what change you should consider, what the implications of that will be, and how to scope and plan for the change.

## CHANGE MANAGER

This role almost needs a chapter of its own. So many times we hear people in the business lament 'It is so hard to find a real change manager'. That of course starts with the assumption that there is such thing as a 'real' change manager, which I am not really comfortable with. It's a term that polarizes and causes umbrage – I maintain that people come from all sorts of disciplines to play critical roles in change, and add significant value, and I get wary of the desire to 'pigeon hole' or create a cookie cutter template of a 'real' change manager.

There is a move to provide accreditations processes for change managers and there's more on that in Chapter 14. But, most simply, a change manager is responsible for: developing a strategy (if one is not done), developing a change plan, designing the implementation of change, and executing the change.

One of the things to consider in thinking about those people who take the role of a change manager is that you will have different levels of change managers, for example, early career or experienced. Early career managers are typically the products of accreditation processes, and the more experienced are more likely to have come from 10+ years of experience backed up with educational qualifications and methodology 'agnostic' when it comes to change tools and frameworks. Both offer value to your organization if you have no change capability.

### CHANGE COMMUNICATIONS ADVISOR

I mentioned before that the change manager will often lead a team. One of the critical roles in the team is the change communication consultant or advisor. This is a person who comes from an organizational communication / employee communication / internal communication background who has specialized in change management. Their independent study or experience within change means they know how to build a communication campaign that will align and support a change program.

For many managers, change communication means fact Sheets, FAQs, Roadshows and Manager Talking Points. Good change communication means timely information that is fed to the troops, providing a consistent message and clarity in meaning.

But others argue for a broader understanding of change communication. Change communication is more than just a tool to introduce the new system, structure or values. A good change communications advisor can connect your messages and intent with the broader narrative of the organization.

## CHANGE ANALYST

Within a change team there is often a change analyst or two, perhaps many depending on the size of the change. A change analyst is a project role that is similar to a business analyst in that they work with large volumes of data. Where they differ is that the change analyst looks at the data through the lens of understanding the audiences of change, the risks of change, and is responsible for producing reports that inform the progress of change. This is often a generalist role and can turn to training analysis, communications analysis and business analysis as required. The change analyst is often the beginning of a career path for change managers.

## CHANGE ENABLERS

This is an often-forgotten community – and it includes teams from communications, HR, and IT functions who inevitably are needed in some capacity to make your change happen. These core functions need to be engaged early in the piece so they can plan for how they can support you. There's no point going to them at the 11th hour and demanding they proof your communications, schedule an intranet article, or address their induction packs. If not treated with respect, they can be change blockers. The good thing about these groups is they are boundary spanners. By that, I mean they span the other projects and activities going on in the organization and so can help you with identifying overlaps, dependencies and schedule based road blocks (e.g., employee engagement survey periods, financial moratoriums).

### SUBJECT MATTER EXPERTS (SMES)

Charmingly pronounced SMEEZ (rhymes with cheese), these are employees identified as having functional expertise. We need to ensure that there is adequate time release from their 'day job' and that their efforts are recognized. They need to get a clear indication of the time requirements throughout the lifecycle of the project. Because of their early exposure on projects, they can be a source of negativity about the change if they are not provided with the context and the rationale of the change or purpose. Similarly, they may also be a great source of enthusiasm as they get advanced opportunity to work through the benefits earlier than others. They may or may not be super users.

### SUPER USERS

Visions of capes and underwear worn on the outside pervade – but these are really just employees identified as having high usage of the impacted processes and systems. This group needs to be provided with additional training and education of a new system and /or process in order to provide support to the rest of the employees when the project goes live. There may be some overlap with change champions, but this is not automatic. They need strong support at the time of 'go live' and for some time after as they will take the brunt of the employees' queries on the changes. One of the risks with super users is that they do not necessarily have the communication and influencing skills to manage the queries they receive at the introduction of a new system. It's often prudent to buddy them up with a change champion. They often need a Lois Lane.

So, there you have it, a little more definition about the roles in change. Perhaps it's now time to gather your team and lead a conversation about the roles you can fill immediately and those that you will need to identify and recruit? The next chapter will help you on that.

### CONVERSATION STARTERS

**Some of the conversations you might want to have right now are:**

- Who do we think should be a change sponsor and who do we think are natural leaders of this change?
- Are there easily identifiable change champions in our business and how might we manage them?
- Is there a difference between change agents and change champions in our business and how does that matter?
- Do we have people in the company who have the experience in change teams – change managers, change analysts?
- Who might we identify as change enablers? SMEs? Or Super users?

## IMPLICATION FOR YOUR CHOICE IN ADVENTURE

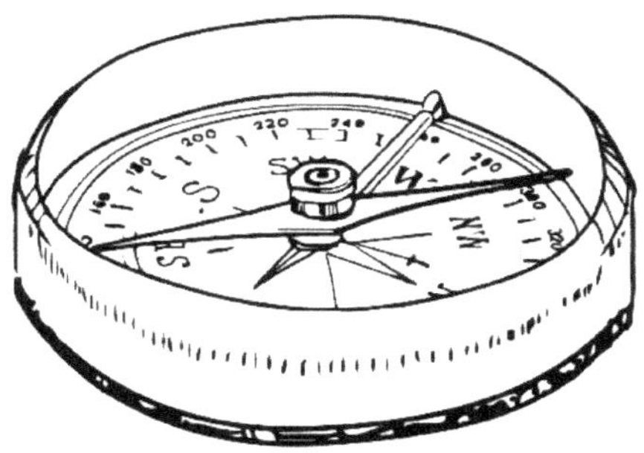

### ADVENTURE 1

- **You do not know what the change is to be,**
- **You have no internal change resources,**
- **You do have budget.**

As you start to change up what the change is likely to be with your change consultant, this will be a handy guide to thinking through who will do what. It will help you to temper considerations of what you are defining is feasible given your resourcing profile.

### ADVENTURE 2

- **You do know what the change is to be,**
- **You have no internal change resources,**
- **You do have budget.**

As you recruit your new team, you know now that you need to recruit not just change managers, but change communicators and change agents. You will also want to give some consideration to change sponsorship and leadership. If this is not you, you will need some-one in this role. Together with your new team you can work through the remainder of the roles and ensure you have them allocated.

### ADVENTURE 3

- **You do know what the change is to be,**
- **You have internal change resources,**
- **You do have budget**

Sometimes when you have internal resources, there are things that are just taken for granted. Using this list in this chapter will help you work through the various roles and ensure that you and your change resources are on the same page.

### ADVENTURE 4

- **You may or may not know what the change is to be,**
- **You have no internal change resources,**
- **You have no budget to hire anyone.**

This chapter may be helpful to you in realizing that you don't have to do it all alone. In understanding the different roles, you may be able to put names to the role and start some influential conversations of seconding people into new positions with you. Ok, yes, I am a Pollyanna.

## THE SECRET IN SECRET CHANGE AGENT, JOE GERGEN

**Is it a bird?** Is it a plane? Is it a change agent?

Is a change agent a job or is it a role? Do we approach change management as a project or is a project endowed with change management?

A true secret change agent has a secret mission. Except that it's not a secret. Anyone can manage a project that will change the organization. The change may be as small as verbiage on a letter template or as sweeping as shutting down a department. But without a secret mission, it's just another disruption to the team members. The role of a secret change agent is to transform every project into something greater by becoming part of the team, by building trust with them so you can promote change from the inside. You are doing the project with them, not to them.

**So what is your mission, should you choose to accept it?**

The key difference between a Secret Change Agent and your runof-the-mill process engineer is the mission. And the mission is to change the culture. It doesn't need to start as radical change – we're not talking 'smash the state' kind of culture change. Think of it more along the lines of 'gradual enlightenment'. With every problem identified, the organization has an opportunity to grow. Our reflex may be to slap a band-aid on the problem and desperately hope the blemish never shows its ugly face again. But the opportunity presented is one of learning. It's not just about solving the problem, but rather about furthering a problem-solving culture. **I love it when a plan comes together**

Every secret mission needs a good plan. Your job is to look at the project and the secret mission and figure out what lessons can be learned about problem-solving. It could be one simple process method. It could be a set of tools to use. It could be feedback loops. You could even be planting seeds for future learning. And as always assess the current capabilities and understanding of the team members. Your job is to set them up to succeed in the learning because that feels good, creates a sense of achievement that they'll want to repeat. **So bring the people in**

By involving the people who live the problem, hopefully the people who identified the problem in the first place, you are taking the first step toward an inclusive learning culture. People are always sensitive about projects and change so it's your job to bring the right attitude. It's your job to guide them not drag them. Take time to understand both the people and the process. Then make an effort to let them know you understand. They'll appreciate that and you'll build the trust necessary to move farther and farther ahead.

First published:https://intothechange.net/2014/02/13/theadventures-of-a-secret-change-agent/

# 4 Perfect Match - more than just a game show

It's often lamented that it's difficult to find a 'real' change manager. One of the reasons is because the people who are looking for change management resources don't understand the field in order to determine who they are looking for (so this book will help you with that one!). Another reason is that people who present as change management resources don't always have the background to do so and it can be difficult to spot the wannabes and the fakes.

This chapter helps you to navigate the selection of your change resources – whether they be an external change consultant, an external change manager, or an internal change resource.

Let's start with the basics: regardless of whether they are internal or external, here is a list of attributes I would be interested in when recruiting an experienced change management resource.

1

They may have a background with one of the 'big 4' or 'big 6' consulting firms (e.g., Deloittes, PWC, Accenture, Ernst and Young) and large corporations who can take a lot of credit for setting up change management practices in the eighties (e.g., IBM, GE, Lotus). These larger firms did a lot of work in the eighties and nineties with academic institutions to develop change management practices, educate clients in the need for OCM, and refine models of change in their consulting wings. Your resources may, however, have come from smaller consultancies or have been working independently within organizations. They can talk to the methodologies they have used in these previous consultancies and they have a default process that guides them through the messiness of human behavior. This default to structure can be a double-edged sword – it will be of enormous benefit in ambiguity and uncertainty. An over-reliance on structure can occur though, to the detriment of empathy and compassion, and ability to build rapport.

2

They probably have undergone a fair bit of professional development in the field. This may look like post-grad qualifications in change management, or they may have professional accreditation such as ACMP, PROSCI, CPI, or CMI. They have invested in their careers as change professionals and have been exposed to many of the thought leaders in their studies or professional development. They read the latest information published, and can compare it to the earlier seminal texts on change and organizational development.

3

They have probably come from one of the following professional backgrounds: Training, HR, Psychology, Engineering, Management, Education, Communications.

4

They are familiar with models of change. They know the pros and cons of many of them, and understand which model or framework is useful for particular situations. A non-exhaustive list to consider would be TQM, Kaizen, Lean, Six Sigma, Appreciative Inquiry, Weisboard's 6 box model, Prosci's ADKAR, Kotter's 8 steps, and PCI. They can make up their own framework to suit the business's needs.

5

They may have formal studies in social psychology, systems thinking, adult learning, strategy development, economics, program management, organizational theory (including structure and process), power, conflict and negotiations, facilitation, coaching, leadership, management, research and analysis, and information technology.

6

They understand that communication is inextricably linked with change. A change manager without an understanding of communication models, methods and tactics will not get you results.

7

While they probably have refined their practice in the pressures of project environments, they can walk into any organization and set out a roadmap for the sequences and stages of change, without having a project manager to answer to.

8

They have very high emotional intelligence and an ability to develop accelerated rapport, and are very flexible. They demonstrate empathy, leadership, and situational wisdom.

9

They have a few years on them. At the risk of sounding ageist, there is a need to have some years of experience behind them. I'd be looking for a minimum of five years and preferably 10 years.

10

They need to be utterly curious and operate with a real passion for the field.

11

They can talk to success and failure in their experiences and what they have learnt from the engagements.

## INTERNAL CHANGE RESOURCES

Depending on the size of your company you may already have a Change Management Office (CMO), or a business unit that provides change management services. If this is the case, you will likely have an established company change methodology. The resources in this unit will often replicate a standard consultancy model – a consultant, a manager, an analyst.

The CMO is typically custodian of:

- Hiring permanent and contract change management resourcing
- Ensuring consistency of change management processes, frameworks and tools
- Maintaining a helicopter view of change in the organization (what else is dropping at what time)
- Prioritization of change efforts for the best impact
- Building change capability through either a formal curriculum or coaching

In many companies, the prioritization of change resources comes through the funding approvals of projects. If you are working through a process where your project has assigned funds, this may trigger a consultation with a change consultant to understand your scope and resourcing needs. Other companies are less formal, and it is a more casual negotiation in that you need to approach the head of change resourcing and alert them to your needs.

It is important to be clear on what you are looking for in a change resource and if you can, ensure you have the right to say no if the resource does not fit your needs. Of course, this only applies if you have the budget to recruit elsewhere!

### EXTERNAL CHANGE CONSULTANTS

In addition to the list above in evaluating what makes for a good change consultant, I would look for some-one who has:

- A breadth of experience

- A deep knowledge of change management
- An ability to develop rapport easily
- A strong network they can call upon for assistance or alternative specialist resources
- Available references or testimonials from clients
- Familiarity with your industry or the type of change to be introduced (it saves time, and time costs with consultants)

Change consultants will usually work on one of three costing models:

- Fixed price
- Time and materials
- Risk and reward

On **fixed price,** the consultant will provide a statement of work with a fixed price for the inclusions in the statement. This is most popular when the scope of the work is clear and there is unlikely to be ongoing work, for example, the consultant will be handing over to a change team internally.

With **time and materials**, the consultant bills based on how much time is spent and any materials (e.g., workshops supplies, catering, diagnostic tools and licensing). This is most often used when the outcome of the change is unknown, the variables are plentiful, and it is difficult to estimate how long it will take.

While **risk and reward** at the outset appears to motivate the consultant to bring about change and align with your goals, risk and reward is the least favored model for consultancies, namely because of how common it is for companies to change their change program. This necessitates a frequent renegotiation of risk and reward, and often takes the result out of the control of the change consultant.

There is a wide variance in consulting fees from Tier 1 consultants (e.g., Deloittes, KPMG, Accenture, PWC) to smaller boutique consulting firms. The process for engaging your consultancy will vary depending on your sourcing and procurement policies and the cost of the engagement. In some companies, there is a strict process and there may even be a list of preferred providers. It is unlikely that that you will find a change consultancy on this list so you may need to make a case with your procurement office as to why you need to go outside of the sourcing and procurement model.

### EXTERNAL CHANGE MANAGERS FOR CONTRACT ENGAGEMENT

A Change Manager for this purpose is bought into an organization in a role that is tactical in nature, usually delivery focused, and often for a discrete piece of work (e.g., as a contractor or a fixed term appointment).

In recruiting an external change manager, you have three options:

1. Word of mouth – asking your trusted professional network who they've worked with and who they would recommend and contacting that person directly.

If you go down this path, you have already signaled to the candidate that they have the value you are looking for and you may find that their rates are higher than those you find through an agency or a job board. It will, however, be a faster process and one with more surety as it's unlikely that your trusted network will provide a bad referral.

2. Using a specialist recruitment agency.

There are recruiting agencies who specialize in change management resourcing and it makes much more sense for you to go through them than through generalist recruiting agencies. They'll have a much stronger network of change management practitioners, know who is available, and what their capabilities are. They are often very adept at helping you define who it is you're looking for. Like all recruiting agencies, they'll charge a percentage for the placement, usually refundable if the candidate is determined not suitable within a set length of time.

3. Open recruiting through a job board or your company's recruiting team.

It may be your company's policy to use your own recruiting team. This may limit you to a preferred layout and stipulation of job ad attributes. Review this chapter with your recruiting team so they understand what the characteristics are of the person you're seeking.

Alternatively, you could just post directly to a job board, although that will have the result of potentially being swamped by candidates. There are a lot of people who think they can do change.

## WHAT DOES CHANGE MANAGEMENT RESOURCING COST?

Change management resources are a specialized asset and as such can appear costly. They tend to be on par with other dedicated project professionals and other consulting fields. Depending on how you intend to resource and how many you require, you could be looking at anywhere from $150,000 (AUD) a person to $4 million (AUD) a year for a large team. A cross check with global peers suggest there is not a huge variability in costs of change resources in the UK, Europe and North America. Depending on your currency you could expect to pay the following:

| Role | Daily rate | Permanent (annual) |
|---|---|---|
| Change Analyst | $550-$700 | $60,000-$125,000 |
| Change Manager | $700-$1000 | $90,000-$150,000 |
| Senior Change Manager | $800-$1,200 | $150,000-$190,000 |

**Table 1.0: Cost of Change Management Resources**

The thing that is very important to do at the outset of your recruiting is to perform a cost benefit analysis. If you can quantify the benefits and the risks of your change that are dependent on usage or adoption, you start to be able to evaluate the return on investment (ROI) of change management. ChangeFirst and PROSCI both have very good whitepapers and online tutorials on how to calculate the ROI of change.The flippant response to what does a change practitioner cost is – what will it cost you to NOT to land the change?

In recent years, we have seen a trend towards fixed term contracts (at the permanent rate). This will work for you if there are not many change initiatives kicking off around you, or you are prepared to take some-one who is early career and ambitious, but not necessarily experienced. The risk / reward ratio is usually not sufficient for an experienced practitioner to do fixed term contracts – that is, it is rare to immediately roll on to another project, in fact you want a change resource to take a break and re-energise. So, the financial implications of taking a three month break every 12 months becomes unattractive.

There is also consideration of what it costs for resources in the non-profit sector. I take a little bit of a contrary position on that – the resources still cost the same. They are not worth less because they work in the third sector. It is up to the change practitioner as to how much of their time they want to donate to do the work. There are many practitioners who get enormous intrinsic reward working with non-profits or charities. Ultimately, in all cases the cost of the change management resource needs to be considered relative to the desired benefits.

## CONVERSATION STARTERS

**Some of the conversations you might want to have right now are:**

- What are the benefits of this initiative in financial terms?
- What percentage of those benefits are dependent on our people making changes to their behavior, adopting new technology or following new processes?
- Are we comfortable with a reduced financial benefit if our people do not adopt the changes?

- If we think about who would be a great cultural fit for our team – what are those attributes?
- What is our thinking on internal versus external resourcing, contractor versus permanent hire or consultant?

### IMPLICATIONS FOR YOUR CHOICE IN ADVENTURE

#### ADVENTURE 1

- **You do not know what the change is to be,**
- **You have no internal change resources,**
- **You do have budget.**

This should provide you with a guide on what to look for in a consultant and some clues on how to engage. Talk with your peers outside of your company to understand who they have used and how effective they were.

#### ADVENTURE 2

- **You do not know what the change is to be,**

- **You have no internal change resources,**
- **You do have budget.**

This should make life a little easier in recruiting your new team. I would be heading to a specialist recruiting firm on this one. Revisit Chapter 3 again to understand the optimum composition of the resources you need to recruit.

## ADVENTURE 3

- **You do know what the change is to be,**
- **You have internal change resources**
- **You do have budget**

This provides a list for you to evaluate your internal resources so you understand their strengths and skills sets. If they don't have the requisite experience and skills, you may need to make a case for external recruiting. Share this chapter with the Resourcing Manager to help facilitate a conversation on who you might be able to have on your team.

## ADVENTURE 4

- **You may or may not know what the change is to be,**
- **You have no internal change resources,**
- **You have no budget to hire anyone.**

The section on calculating ROI may be useful to you in revisiting the need for a budget and then how to recruit. Failing that, use the attribute list to think about who exists in the organization at the moment who meets those attributes – you may have an ally lurking around.

Footnote: this list was refined through conversations with members of the Organizational Change Professionals Group on LinkedIn – it's a wonderful source of knowledge and wisdom in this field.

## CONVERSATIONS OF CHANGE WITH ALAN HERRITY, DIRECTOR, MOMENTUM SEARCH AND SELECTION

**Dr. Jen:** I thought it would be really interesting to have a chat about recruiting in the change management field. In Australia, in particular, we have probably about five to six specialist recruiting agencies that focus specifically on organizational change management and placing change practitioners. But, we also have your generalist recruiting companies who might happen to advertise for a change manager but without really understanding anything about what the role is, or the candidates, or what the client's needs are. To that point, now I seem to recall that you did a PCI change accreditation piece. Is that correct?

**Alan:** Yes, in September 2013 I did the PCI change management practitioner course. And the reason why I did that is that I think it is important to invest into organizational change management as an industry. I think it has really helped me with conversations with both clients and candidates. And I also think it helps from a credibility perspective.

**Dr. Jen:** So, if I can start with: What do you think are some of the trends that you're seeing in recruiting change managers in the Australian market at the moment?

**Alan:** I think there is a trend towards permanent roles especially at that senior level, which tells me that organizations are looking to build capability and keep that change management role in-house, and keep the IP within the organization. So, I think that's a good thing.

**Dr. Jen:** Interesting, do you think that there are consistent themes that you see in terms of challenges in that recruiting process or the interview process?

**Alan:** Yeah, I think so. I remember a few years ago a senior executive said to me, 'all those change practitioners, all of their CVs look the same'. And then he said 'Alan, you need to help me with that, and you need to help everybody else by helping them change their CV'. And I understand where he was coming from. I think in terms of how organizations interview change practitioners, there is a lot of work that needs to be done.

**Dr. Jen:** How so?

**Alan:** Well I think there needs to be an alignment between the business and speaking to the acquisition (procurement) department if they have one, and the agencies, if they use an external agency, in terms of what does 'good' look like? What do I need from a change practitioner? There seems to be still a lot of people out there saying that they need a change practitioner but they don't seem to be sure why. And they will ask project related questions which are more in line with project delivery or communications, or training related questions, which is not the entirety of what a change practitioner would do. You also find on the market in the change world that a lot of clients are looking for subject matter experts or specialist transformation knowledge in the change practitioner, whether that would be in an ERP or digital transformation.

**Dr. Jen:** Okay, so you see it all the time in digital that you must have experience in digital transformation to be a digital change manager.

**Alan:** Yeah and in my humble opinion that's not necessary because you should have the digital experts with the organization who can bring the subject matter expertise and the change manager works with them.

**Dr. Jen:** It does introduce a really interesting binary experience there really, in thinking of myself as a change practitioner, to switch between 'well here is my expertise and what I know about digital' to 'here is what I know about change management'. It's almost like you're sacrificing one for the other when you bring in a change manager as a Subject Matter Expert (SME).

**Alan:** Yeah, I think so. Like yourself, I like to write blogs. One of the blogs I'm thinking about is 'change practitioner or project manager – which do I need?' There seems to be a trend like that over the last couple of years on the market, where the market's got a little bit tighter. So, organizations are being picky and they are looking for 'unicorns' with regard to practitioners. They have a bit of a wish list around the sort of skills and experiences that they want and they want the change practitioner and the project manager in the one candidate.

And they want subject matter expertise as well. I think it's important for talent acquisition and recruiting agencies to push back on that. I don't understand why there is an insistence on subject matter expertise. What is it about that subject matter expertise which will make that person successful and grow in a change role? And I understand the explanation that it will make the stakeholders feel comfortable but that's still not a good enough reason for you to hire somebody without subject matter expertise, because if somebody has got subject matter expertise, they will tend to just focus and maybe be blinkered around the subject matter expertise. While a change practitioner will bring a lot of breadth and a lot of different views on how to handle a change and a transformation initiative rather than just focusing on the subject matter expertise.

**Dr Jen:** So, you mentioned the unicorn there in terms of the client requirements. My favourite at the moment is the 'slashie'. So, we want the change manager [slash] project manager. How do you handle requests like that when they come through from client? Do you try and seek that person or do you actually push back and look at the issues associated with it?

**Alan:** I think it's a good question, because I was with a client recently and they are a smaller organization and they can't afford to have a number of change practitioners on board. So they got a few change practitioners, but what they did was they actually trained up all their project managers as change practitioners. So, the projects that the change practitioners can't get to, the change managers are at least looking at how they make this project successful from a change and project perspective. So, I think that's not actually a bad approach if the organization can't afford to bring in several change practitioners.

Some of the organizations are smaller than most. I think with the little organizations I was trying to get an understanding of, okay, well why did they need somebody to be a 'slashie' and be able to do both? How has that worked for them previously? Because if you get an understanding of that, well then you can get an understanding of if they want a project manager who is just really good with communications and training or do they really want a proper change practitioner. That's where you could tend to understand what the requirements really are or maybe push back on the clients and explain to them what a real change practitioner brings versus a project manager.

**Dr. Jen:** The position I come to you with that is I don't deny or disagree that someone can be a 'slashie', they can do both things in terms of someone who is a change manager can be quite skilled as a project manager, and is often required to use project management skills. Someone who is a very good project manager may also be a very good change manager. The issue that I have is that it's very challenging to do both under one engagement, something gives and it's kind of like you get 50% performance in both arenas, when you need 100%.

**Alan:** And I think also from a recruiters' perspective, we place both project and change roles. I'd say, arguably, the project role is easier to place because it's more black and white, it's more about delivery. Don't get me wrong, you know stakeholder management, trouble shooting and problem solving, all of the little things that a good project or program practitioner need will, for me, be change management. But it's quite a lot of 'grey' and a lot of ambiguity, and the best change practitioners on the market can deal with that and roll with the punches and help the organization move from an ambiguous situation to the new state of whatever that would be – whether it's leadership piece or re-structure role or a technology project for example.

**Dr. Jen:** So, you've told us a little bit about the challenges from a client perspective. What about from the candidate perspective, what do they talk to you about in terms of what's challenging in the interview processes or engagements?

**Alan:** I think mostly it's about the understanding of what a change practitioner brings. So they might have questions around communications, training, and their individual roles. And a change practitioner can do elements of those roles but that's not necessarily what a change practitioner would bring on a change initiative for me. I think there is an opportunity, and a need, for someone in talent acquisition or procurement to work with change practitioners in their organizations to understand how to recruit change practitioners. And for those change practitioners to potentially educate the business or procurement and talent acquisition.

**Dr Jen:** How long do you think it will take to achieve that level of education, and is that your role (as recruiter) or is the onus on the client to skill themselves up? Where do you fit in that?

**Alan:** I think it's part of my role. I think it's about building partnerships and relationships. I think it takes a while and it's a big investment for organization but, if you're serious about change, I think it is important to do. People have said that 'change is the new constant', so if we're constantly changing, we need to be making sure that we're bringing the right people into the organization and we know how to do that.

**Dr Jen:** So when you meet someone at a barbecue or a party and you tell them what you do and they say 'oh I've been thinking of getting into change' or 'that looks like a really interesting career', do you give them any particular counsel or advice?

**Alan:** Yeah that's an interesting one. I always try and understand their reasoning for going into change because it's important not to jump on the bandwagon just because it's a shiny new toy. You need to understand why you want to do it, and to be passionate about that area. Whatever that may be.

I think for somebody who is quite junior, certification is not a bad idea. It certainly helped me and gave me some insights. And then just making sure that you go into the right networking groups, and get into the right events – like Change Management Professionals for example.

You're meeting the right people. So, try and really immerse yourself into those areas and get as much experience as possible.

# 5 Start with the end in mind

Okay, so far, you've worked your way through some of the core components of the domain of change management, gained some clarity on who are the key characters in change, and considered who you need and how you might recruit them. Before you go any further you should spend some time framing up what success will look like for you.

You really can't go past Stephen Covey's classic principle 'Start with the End in Mind' when shaping up success. Successful change for me involves three elements: clarity of purpose, understanding of the enablers of success, and the ability to measure that success. They form a three-legged platform of change. When you lose one of them, things get a little unstable. Let's consider each one.

## PURPOSE

We hear a lot of the 'why' of change being important, but I think the rationale for change can be very different to purpose. The rationale or 'why' of change is the objective that drives the initiative. We are doing this because we want to reduce operational expenses. We are doing this because we want to become more customer centric / innovative / insert buzzword of the day. We are doing this to enable better management of our records. When presented with an objective of change it is often easy to say, 'so what?'

Purpose goes deeper than that. Purpose is the thing that people will get out of bed for, that they will work long hours for, that they will take risks for. If you get purpose right, it's harder to say, 'so what?' Purpose is meaningful and enduring. Purpose speaks to personal identity and organizational mission. It drives the 'why' of what your organization does. Or should do.

At this point, the concept of purpose is either immediately obvious to you, you've got it and you know it because you are already living a purposeful working life in a company that is purpose driven. It is easy to articulate your change objective in context of the organization's purpose that the employees embrace.

Or it is incredibly nebulous and you realise you have never stopped to think about it. And perhaps this is raising some uncomfortable feelings. And you know what? That's fantastic. If after some serious rumination, you cannot articulate the purpose, then stop moving forward on the change. It will fall over. Or at the least not be sustainable or yield the benefits you are hoping for.

## UNDERSTANDING OF THE ENABLERS OF SUCCESS

No doubt when you first started talking to people about your intent to drive this change, you would have heard some folk talk about how hard change is. They may have thrown out statistics that show that the vast majority of change fails. And you may have thought 'what have I done?' Well, at the end of this chapter I unpack the '70% of change fails' myth, but for, now what I propose is listing the elements that enable successful change.

It's a long list – and to that end those who say change is hard are correct. One of the foundation fathers of change management is Kurt Lewin, and he is most well-known for his three phases of change – unfreezing, changing, and refreezing. And while this is a relatively useful way of looking at change from a helicopter view, it tells you little about how to change in the real world. It's not a simple three step process, and there's no fail-safe recipe. You do need to mix the ingredients to suit your diners!

The elements I have seen contribute to successful change are:

- Clarity of purpose and the change objective
- Clarity of understanding of the current state, the future state, and the size of the gap (across systems, processes, behaviours)
- People to lead change
- People to drive change
- People to manage change
- Project teams that are resourced to make the change happen
- The end-user or audience being involved in the design of the change (i.e., not having it thrust upon them)
- A culture that values learning and is comfortable with ambiguity and uncertainty
- Strong communication not just of the change, but during the change
- Programs designed to build the audience's readiness to change

I used the recipe analogy above, and to some extent you do get to be the creative chef in this. So, for example, if you do not have enough clarity of understanding of the current state, the future state and the size of the gap, you can still be successful with a culture that values learning and is comfortable with ambiguity and uncertainty and some strong people to lead change. Clarity becomes emergent in the process.

If you do not have a lot of clarity of purpose and the change objective, you can get across the line with strong communication and early involvement of stakeholders in the design. Purpose becomes emergent in the process.

While my counsel is to consider the elements of change success before you get started, this is a great list to review on a periodic basis as a health check before you need take remedial action.

## ABILITY TO MEASURE SUCCESS

When I talk to leaders and steering committees about change success I use three categories to understand change success metrics – installation, benefits realization, and process of change. If you are not considering these before you start your change, you will not be able to evaluate how you are going.

Measuring the success of the 'installation' of a change can occur pretty shortly after 'go live', whereas the other two can occur prior to go live and at periodic intervals post go live. But a consideration first of project success and its relationship to change success.

### Project success

Most of the change projects we work are deemed successful by project success measures like IFOTOB (delivered In Full, On Time, On Budget). But this alone is not sufficient. I think we can all think of projects where it looked good from a delivery perspective but user adoption was low and the benefits were limited. From a change management perspective, I tend to be interested in this but not ruled by it. Ultimately, changes in scope, time delays and cost blow outs create a lot more stakeholder engagement and expectation management. You want to contribute to a strong result here, but it really does not measure the success of the change.

### User adoption / employee compliance

User adoption tends to be used in technology / systems implementation, and talks about 'to what extent does the user adopt the new system and its features?' You can also consider employee compliance in the same bucket. Does anything actually change? Are people using the new system, are they behaving in a new way? Are they using new processes? Successful installation is dependent on something actually changing!

I know this sounds obvious – but it's a real oversight in the change success discussions. Often the discussions focus on benefits realization, and if the benefits are not achieved it can be argued that the change management team did not do a good enough job and needs to improve its practice! But the reasons behind low benefits realization are many and varied – for example, the change team may have had great installation results, but the original logic behind the change was flawed and wasn't sustainable.

It's in this category that traditional change readiness surveys / polls come in handy. Being able to poll for 'will they [make the change] and can they [make the change] pre-go live' puts you in a much stronger place at time of installation. You can target your efforts with remediation or intervention to ensure a good user adoption / employee compliance measurement.

Ultimately, you are looking for metrics on log-ins of the new system, new processes being followed, calls to support structures decreasing (or increasing). Common sense tells you 100% adoption on Day One is unlikely, but with some careful thought, you can identify a baseline metric for the current state and expected usage or compliance over time.

#### Benefits realization

It's a rare change initiative where you can measure benefits realization immediately after going live. If you can, then you were working on something that was pretty broken to start with! Benefits often take some time to start to become apparent. This can be because it takes time for new habits to form with behavioural change, proficiency to increase with systems usage, or business cycles to play out.

The time of things you are looking to measure here are tangible measures – speed to market, cost of transaction, cycle time, Full Time Employee (FTE) release, speed of processes, and employee engagement increase.

It can help to think about your benefits in stages – so at 30 days post-installation or go-live, the date at which you launch your change, what would you expect to see that would suggest things are tracking well. At 60 days? At 90 days? Sometimes you need to consider what you can't see and hear as success. In organizational environments that are known for vocal opposition to change, sometimes measuring 'silence' tells you something about success.

### Change process success

It is very informative to measure how effective the actual change process was. Nothing kills a future change faster than the legacy of poorly executed change. Some of the things that we can consider along the way are periodic assessments of where people are on the change curve (awareness, understanding, buy-in, commitment). Do the people feel empowered?

And then the one that really makes a difference is the 'campsite rule'. Think about nature conservationists – they implore us to leave the campsite in a better state than when we got there. The same goes for change management. Really successful change management means that you've built change capability and considered sustainable change. Your organization has a higher state of change maturity at the end of your change initiative than before you started.

Personally, I don't think it matters what the metrics are that you decide on as much as that you have this conversation with those that matter.

It can be incredibly powerful to have a rich discussion on what success looks like with organizational leaders, the steering committee and project teams to align expectations and education about change management. Only then can we move away from the puffery of '70% of change projects fail' and start to have conversations that yield better results of change.

## SO, YES, ABOUT THAT 70% CHANGES FAIL 'STATISTIC'. IT'S A LOAD OF CODSWALLOP.

A few years ago, business academic Mark Hughes published a compelling critique of the '70% of Change Fails' and it validated what a few of us in the industry had been thinking – that it can't be true! I wrote a lengthy blog post on it which you can easily find and have done a few talks on the topic, but the essence of it as follows:

Once upon a time in a galaxy far, far away…. In 1993 Professor Michael Hammer and consulting firm chairman James Champy publish the book 'Re-engineering the Corporation'. This is based on research on Business Process Re-engineering (BPR) initiatives. BPR initiatives in the 80's and 90's meant very large organizational changes. The book contains success case studies of IBM, Ford Motor Company, Hallmark and Taco Bell. But what resonates with the business community is the following statement:

Sadly, we must report that despite the success stories described in previous chapters, many companies that begin reengineering don't succeed at it… Our unscientific estimate is that as many as 50 per cent to 70 per cent of the organizations that undertake a reengineering effort do not achieve the dramatic results they intended. (Hammer and Champy, 1993, p. 200)

An 'unscientific estimate'. No definitions of success. No investigation of validity of expectations. **70% of BPR projects fail.** Sexy stuff, people.

In 1996, Professor John Kotter publishes the article 'Leading Change' in the Harvard Business Review. Rather than quote studies, he notes he has 'observed' over 100 companies in the previous ten years with success varying. He is circumspect about success and failure rates, noting the varying stages and reasons for difficulty. Kotter's 1996 work is often referenced as a source of the 70% Change fail statistic. It's not in this article. The eight-step framework is in this one.

In 2000, researchers Michael Beer and Nitin Nohria publish 'Cracking the Code of Change' in the Harvard Business Review (HBR). The article is about their work on Theory O and Theory E of change. But the sentence that grabs the attention of the consulting world is almost a throwaway line at the beginning:
'The brutal fact is that about 70% of all change initiatives fail.' (Beer and Nohria, 2000, p. 133).

Nothing to support it, no mention of where this fact has come from, how the figure has emerged to be a 'brutal fact'. But it does set up a need for an alternative theory of change (e.g., Theory E and Theory O).

From an academic perspective, Mark Hughes published a fascinating challenge to the statistic in the Journal of Change Management in 2011. From his analysis, many of the subsequent published papers form a version of a set of academic matryoshka dolls. Examination of their proof of the 70% citation inevitably leads to Hammer and Champy and Beer and Nohria. The mind boggles how many times this statistic has set up a justification for the academics' following endeavours. Indeed, he notes that Michael Hammer has distanced himself from the original statement.

Unfortunately, this simple descriptive observation has been widely misrepresented and transmogrified and distorted into a normative statement . . . There is no inherent success or failure rate for reengineering. (Hammer and Stanton, 1995, p. 14, cited in Hughes, 2011).

These two sources (Hammer and Champy, and Beer and Nohria) made the curriculum reading lists of pretty much every undergrad and postgrad in the western world. And thus, influenced a very large cohort of managers, consultants, project managers and change management practitioners.

The figure gets a life of its own. In 2008 in 'A Sense of Urgency', Professor John Kotter 'estimates' more than 70% of needed change fails. His website states 'Thirty years of research by leadership guru Dr John Kotter has proven that 70% of all major change efforts in organizations fail'. I understand that someone who researches in the area may be reluctant to challenge this and ask to see the research to evaluate its design. Some sacred cows you don't touch…

From an academic perspective, you have a choice at this point. Do you position against famous professors with best-selling books and challenge the 'unscientific' statement and 'estimates'? To challenge Beer and Nohria on the 'brutal fact' is to distract from what is a pretty useful theory and contribution to change (Theory X and Theory O). Maybe you need to wait twenty years to do so. It may be more prudent for career progression to stand on the shoulders of giants and build incremental 'knowledge' on 70% failure rates.

So, then large consulting firms and IT vendors get in on the act. Somewhere along the line some pretty good studies on project implementation and benefits get further twisted into a persistent myth that 70% of all change projects fail. Statistics like that can be very useful in selling services and products. They create fear. If you don't use our services, you may be in the 70% … that would be bad.

Industry heavyweights and thought leaders continue to popularise the statistic with Daryl Conner using it as a big stick to beat up change practitioners and admonish them to do better. (Why after 30 years are we still having 70% of our change projects fail? We must be culpable). Ron Ashkenas recently used it in the HBR again. This means it must be true.

But it's not. And here are six reasons why:

1. The definition of 'change project' is questionable – if it's not resourced with change practitioners, and uses a change methodology, can you claim it was a change project?

2. The definition of 'success' is questionable. 100% successful? 90%? 70%?
3. Success is measured at the wrong time. As noted above, there will be different success criteria and timing for inflight change, installation and benefits realization.

4. The units of analysis are not the same. The multiple studies reference different types of companies, industries and types of change.

5. I don't think I'm [that] special, nor my peers. For this statistic were to be true, I would have 70% of my change initiatives shelved as failures. So, would my peers. We don't.

6. A Career Limiting Admission for a CEO. Seriously. You want me to believe that 70% of the world's CEOs have led failed change efforts? Even if the surveys are anonymous, somewhere there are 70% of company boards looking at poor performances from their CEOs. I struggle with that.

What does this mean to you?

Don't be afraid of change. 70% do not fail. Change can be difficult, but if you resource it well, are clear on how you are going to measure success, and keep track of those metrics and take corrective measures if needed, you will be fine. I promise.

## CONVERSATION STARTERS

**Some of the conversations you might want to have right now are:**

- What is your personal purpose? Your organization's purpose? Why do you exist? How does this change align with the purpose of the organization?
- What does success look like to you at the moment?
- How will success be paced? What are the different ways of measuring success at different points?

## IMPLICATIONS FOR YOUR CHOICE IN ADVENTURE

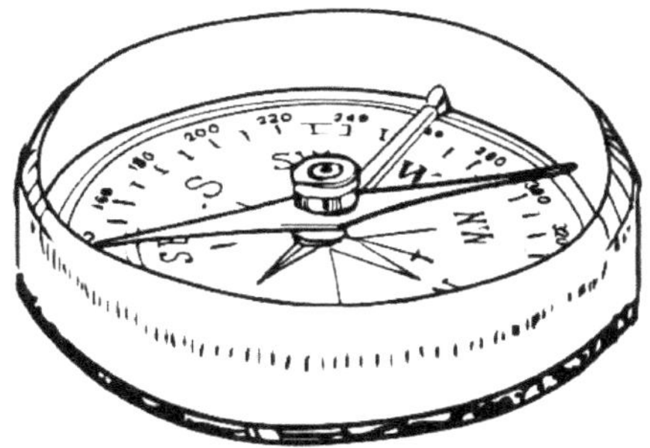

### ADVENTURE 1

- **You do not know what the change is to be,**
- **You have no internal change resources,**
- **You do have budget.**

In this instance, purpose becomes your true North. As you navigate your way through the initial conversations of change, shaping up the design of the solution to your problem, you will benefit from regularly checking the alignment to purpose.

If you are unclear what the change is, it is important consider milestone-based success measures. It will be difficult to establish an installation or benefits realization metric upfront. This will become clearer as you progress though. Initially, you will want to focus on the process of change as your area to measure. In working through the uncertainty and ambiguity, how are your people feeling? What is the level of contribution you are seeing?

What are the implications of all of this talk about change on their productivity?

## ADVENTURE 2

- **You do know what the change is to be,**
- **You have no internal change resources,**
- **You do have budget.**

You're starting with clarity on the change to be implemented, which can be very useful. But have you leaped ahead without considering purpose? If the change makes no sense to your people from a heart and soul level, success is going to be challenged. As you recruit and on board your change resources, the definition of success needs to be an overt and open conversation with them as ultimately, how you define the success of your initiative becomes their performance metrics (e.g., are they effective in achieving these results). Be very clear that the metric you are using for change is aligned with the duration of time you have them around – if you have not included them in the design of the change, it is less likely you can measure their performance with the success of your change. Similarly, if they are contractors or internal resources who are not around to do the embedding work, it is unfair to align their performance metrics with your benefit realization.

## ADVENTURE 3

- **You do know what the change is to be,**
- **You have internal change resources,**
- **You do have budget.**

You, too, need to do a quick check on alignment with purpose. You are all set up to go, but it will be a false start if the change is not aligned with the broader purpose of the organization.

Check with your internal resources on how they have measured success in the past. It may be that measuring success is unfamiliar to them and it will be useful to go through the ROI exercise to formulate messaging for your stakeholders on why this is initiative is so important (e.g., the costs of not doing it). Do lead a conversation with them on what they have seen work well in the organization before – what is the optimum recipe for success?

## ADVENTURE 4

- **You may or may not know what the change is to be,**
- **You have no internal change resources,**
- **You have no budget to hire anyone.**

So, I'm guessing someone has a pretty strong agenda for change to put you in this position. Change must happen. Start with that person and have a conversation on what the purpose of the organization is and how does that align with the need to change, and the ability to not resource the change. If that conversation fails to change your circumstances then you need to look at the enablers of success with an eye for frugal ingredients.

You can still measure success – it may be that your success is just more modest than others. Reality checks will be very important.

# 6 The adventure begins – frameworks and models

OK, sleeves rolled up, let's get moving. You've got a good sense of what this field is about, how you should resource your initiative, and how to set yourself up for success. Let's move on to what model or framework you should use.

One of the things I hear frequently is people talking about change management as being something new. I think if we look at history and the organization we see that change management is not new at all. Even today, one of the claims that is often made is 'The only constant is change' (Heraclitis, 535BC-435BC). Niccolo Machiavelli noted: '... there is nothing more difficult and dangerous, or more doubtful of success, than an attempt to introduce a new order of things...' ('The Prince', 1513).

If you trace the evolution of management theory, you will see that each paradigm of management dealt with change management, albeit often with a singular focus. Scientific Management (Taylorism) during 1880-1920 dealt with task-focused change to improve efficiency. Later popularised by his 1922 essay 'Bureaucratization', Weber laid out the principles for structural change. The Humans Relations approach initiated in the 1920s focused more on making changes that addressed how people related to their roles and colleagues. The Social Technical Systems (STS) approach in the 1950s dealt more with addressing the interdependencies of systems, technology and people.

What is perhaps new is the focus on change management as a profession and the charging of money for the knowledge on how to change companies. I would argue that this practice emerged from the 1980s and we can thank the Big 6 consulting groups and Daryl Conner (one of the industry's most influential change management experts) for the commodification of Change Management intellectual property.

It was at this time too that many of the core publications that made it to managers' desks emerged:

- Rosabeth Moss Kanter, The Change Masters, 1983
- Peter Senge, The Fifth Discipline, 1990
- William Bridges, Managing Transitions, 1991
- Hammer and Champy, BPR Re-engineering the Corporation, 1993
- Daryl Conner, Managing at the Speed of Change, 1993
- John Kotter, Leading Change, 1996
- Spencer Johnson, Who Moved My Cheese, 1998

The 90s saw Positive Psychology start to create a strong influence in the field, and by the 2000s, we had a wide proliferation of change models and frameworks in existence. This period also saw the multiplying of change initiatives – where before, an organization might have gone through a major change once every three to five years, the tempo of change increased so that as the new century took flight, most organizations were undergoing continuous changes on a regular and often relentless basis.

You'll find a plethora of models and frameworks available for you to use. Many are generated after much research; some are generated simply as something to license and make some money from.

In thinking about the utility of certain change models, and why, even if you have one, change can be still hard to do, I recalled an academic paper from a while ago. It struck me that it explained the conundrum well. Let me run it by you.

Karl Weick was the academic who wrote the piece. Weick was one of my absolute favourites to study. He's an organizational theorist who writes on sense-making (among other things). He is super storyteller, and his academic writing is incredibly easy to read. If you get the chance, check out his paper 'The Collapse of Sensemaking in Organizations: The Mann Gulch Disaster', in Administrative Science Quarterly, Vol. 38. At the risk of sounding very nerdy, 16 years later when I catch up with friends from uni days we still discuss his concepts at dinners and BBQs. Yep, okay. A bit too nerdy?

Anyhow, the article I am thinking of tells of the trade-off in writing good theory: 'Conclusion: Theory Construction as Disciplined Reflexivity: Trade-offs in the 90s' in The Academy of Management Review, Vol. 24, No. 4, Oct., 1999, pp. 797-806. In it, Weick argues there is a trade-off in theory development of three attributes: generalizability, accuracy, and simplicity. He suggests you can only ever get two of the three.

Hang with me.

So, for instance, a theory that is simple and accurate can't be generalizable to the greater population. A theory that is simple and general will never be accurate. A theory that is accurate and general is going to be very complex.

Got it? Of course, change models and change frameworks are simply extensions of theory, right?

Simplicity in change models is easy to align – any of the 3 steps, 8 steps, 5 stages are representative of simple models.

Accuracy is less easy to define. For me, it speaks of comprehensive, complicated and nuanced change models – considering multiple contextual factors. I don't know of many change models that do that to be honest.

And general suggests one size fits all. Something that can apply to most change. Many of them do that.

So, it stands to reason that a change model that is simple and general won't be accurate (or comprehensive). A change model that is accurate (comprehensive) and generalised to many situations is going to be very complicated. And the change model that is simple and accurate – well it might just be a one-off, right? Industry specific? Magic happens…

I've found that anything that is simple and general has needed a lot of tweaking and adapting to make it work for the circumstances. Which is the reason why you want to get an experienced change practitioner to work with you. They should have enough experience to tailor generic change models and frameworks to your specific circumstance. Better still, they know when to drop the model or framework when your feedback tells you it is not fit for purpose.

Kelvin Hard, Chairman of Kairos Management Consultants in the UK articulates it well with a musician's metaphor:

*Change management frameworks can be useful in helping change leaders and change teams to have a sense of what is going on. But their limiting factor is when an issue arises which is not covered by the framework, or at a different stage from when the framework says it is 'supposed' to occur. A top change consultant will know and access the frameworks but be able to move beyond them when the context demands. Here is a musical analogy. A good, trained musician will be able to play a set piece of music by following the notes. A great musician will be able to 'play jazz': to play a set of notes which have never been played before (and never will again) but which are just right for that specific time and place.*

So, with those concepts in place – simple, general and accurate in place – let's review six of the models you have available to you. They are all relatively simple and general. Accuracy is up to how you use contextualise them.

## THE PROSCI ADKAR MODEL

Prosci's ADKAR model is by far the most popular today and used across multiple countries and regions. ADKAR represents five milestones that an individual should achieve if successful change is to occur.

- Awareness of the need for change
- Desire to participate in and support the change

- Knowledge on how to change
- Ability to implement required skills and behaviours
- Reinforcement to sustain the change

Supplementing this is a three-phase change process:

1. Prepare for Change
2. Manage Change
3. Reinforce the Change

Prosci was founded by Jeff Hiatt. You are required to be certified in it before you can say you use the Prosci process. It has a suite of tools and templates associated with it. It's globally recognised and companies are licensed to provide the certification and training by Prosci.

Most of the organizations that I have worked in that use Prosci don't use it beyond ticking off ADKAR in their change plan. It's a safety net – 'we have people who are accredited in Prosci, we'll be right'. That's not to diminish the value of the methodology. I think it is a strong one. You also get access to contemporary research with best practice reports, webinars, online communities and ongoing product development.

Certification in use of the methodology will set you back just under $6000 AUD and take three days. Try reading Jeff Hiatt's book first ADKAR (How to Implement Successful Change in Our Personal Lives and Professional Careers) to see if it resonates.

## CHANGEFIRST'S PCI (PEOPLE CENTERED IMPLEMENTATION)

The other change framework that is taking purchase is PCI – from Changefirst. Also, international, it relies on six Critical Success Factors.

The change methodology is also supplemented by a cloud-based on-line community (eChange). Like Prosci, Changefirst offers white papers, workshops, training and research.

It will also cost you $3500 AUD, including a three years subscription to the 'e-change' platform, and take three days to do – try downloading the white papers from Changefirst to get a sense of how it works with your organization.

## KOTTER'S 8 STEPS

So often you may see in recruiting advertisements companies wanting people who are certified in Kotter's 8 steps. While a few training providers can be found to offer a 'Leading Change Certification' based on his work, his company does not offer a Leading Change Certification or something that is endorsed by them. And it shows you why you are not alone in feeling lost in all of the gobbledegook on the web! What Kotter International does offer is their eight-step change process as outlined in Kotter's 1996 book Leading Change. The eight steps are:

### Creating a climate for change

1. Increasing urgency

2. Building the guiding team

3. Getting the right vision

**Engaging the enabling organization**

4. Communicate for buy-in

5. Empower action

6. Create short-term wins

**Implementing and sustaining change**

7. Don't let up

8. Make it stick

More recently, Kotter International has adapted this to reflect more contemporary versions of change as published in his recent book Accelerate. Kotter's process is very good if you take the time to read his books and understand the nuances of the 'steps' and if (and only if), you recognise that it is not a sequential process. It is iterative and concurrent. Simply applying the eight steps above will not take you very far as you miss the detail and caveats.

## BESPOKE FRAMEWORKS

If you are in a very large organization, you may have your own change process. It will be some derivation of the ones above and a generic project methodology. I often think bespoke change frameworks for organizations work much better as it means that someone in a relatively high level has cared enough to think through what the organization needs, and this gives you real senior buy-in for successful change. Maybe by the end of this book you will feel empowered to draft your own?

## APPRECIATIVE INQUIRY

Appreciative inquiry was developed by academics David Cooperrider and Suresh Srivasta, and advanced by work from Cooperrider and Diana Whitney. It turns traditional deficit based change on its head.

What I mean by that is, usually, change management starts AFTER you have identified something is not working well and/or is broken. This can be very dispiriting for all involved, and often hard for the people who have contributed to the brokenness to acknowledge and take responsibility for. Do it often enough in an organization and you have an epidemic of change fatigue.

Appreciative Inquiry starts from a very different point. In acknowledging an appetite for change, the facilitator asks questions that are based on appreciating and positive regard. If you wanted to increase sales in an organization, you would ask people to share stories of the best sales performer they have ever witnessed. What was it they did, they said, they believed. And in eliciting the 'secret sauce' from those who are admired as representative of the best that can be in the organization, you then look to replicate that. It shifts the energy considerably and I must say this is one of my biases. The basic frame work is Discover – Dream – Design – Destiny. A lot of the time people think Appreciative Inquiry needs to be done in a large group intervention. I find if it is your fundamental philosophy behind change, it fuels all your small conversations one-on-one and these can make a big difference.

Cooperrider and Whitney in their 2001 article distinguish between the traditional Problem Solving view of change and the positive psychology approach.

| **Problem Solving** | **Appreciative Inquiry** |
|---|---|
| **Basic Assumption**: An Organization is a Problem to be Solved | **Basic Assumption**: An Organization is a Mystery to be Embraced |
| 1. 'Felt Need,' Identification of Problem | 1. Appreciating and Valuing the Best of 'What Is' |
| 2. Analysis of Causes | 2. Envisioning 'What Might Be' |
| 3. Analysis and Possible Solutions | 3. Dialoguing 'What Should Be' |
| 4. Action Planning (Treatment) | 4. Designing 'What Can Be' |

**Table 2.0: Difference between traditional change approach and Appreciative Inquiry**

Typically, you will use a four-step process to elicit positive responses.

1. DISCOVER: The identification of organizational processes that work well.
2. DREAM: The envisioning of processes that would work well in the future.
3. DESIGN: Planning and prioritising processes that would work well.
4. DESTINY (or DEPLOY): The implementation (execution) of the proposed design.

## AGILE OR LEAN CHANGE

Much to the chagrin of many change practitioners, there isn't a formal Agile or Lean Change methodology per se. A formal agile change methodology is counter to the philosophy of Agile.

There are, however, many values, practices and activities that originate from Agile and Lean or Kaizen methodologies that can be used within change projects. Some practitioners have developed methodologies from those principles and practices and will offer training in them.

They tend to focus on increased communication and collaborative activity and a tendency to move towards co-creation with the audiences who are the intended recipients of change. There's a strong emphasis on hypothesis driven interventions where continuation of the change, or amplification of the change, depends on feedback from small experiments (or pilots). This means that if you get feedback that it's not working you can redirect your efforts.

## SUMMARY

So, these are the change models and frameworks that I am seeing as popular at the moment. This is by far a non-exhaustive list! Of the change methodologies, you may want to do extra research on: GE CAP, Beckhard and Harris Change Management Process, BCG Change Delta, Bridges Transition Model, Change Leaders Roadmap (Anderson and Anderson), LaMarsh Managed Change, and then each of the big consulting firms (Deloittes, Accenture, PWC, IBM) have their own proprietary change model.

And if you want to take it to another level again, do a search on SlideShare for Mark Simpson's Taxonomy of Change Related Models. You will find *47* of them categorised by whether they are:

- Contextual (a broader strategic of macro model that is helpful in understanding the context of change)
- High level change – broad and conceptual
- Actionable – with detailed steps and actions
- Supporting – models that under pin an approach to change.

Almost sounds like simple, general and accurate, right?

## CONVERSATION STARTERS

**Some of the conversations you might want to have right now are:**

- Do we have a change model or framework that is well regarded in our organization?
- Do we have any resources that are certified in a particular model?
- How much time do we have to think about contextualising a changeTo what extent is our workforce change fatigued and may benefit from appreciative inquiry?
- How structured should our change be?

## IMPLICATIONS FOR YOUR CHOICE IN ADVENTURE

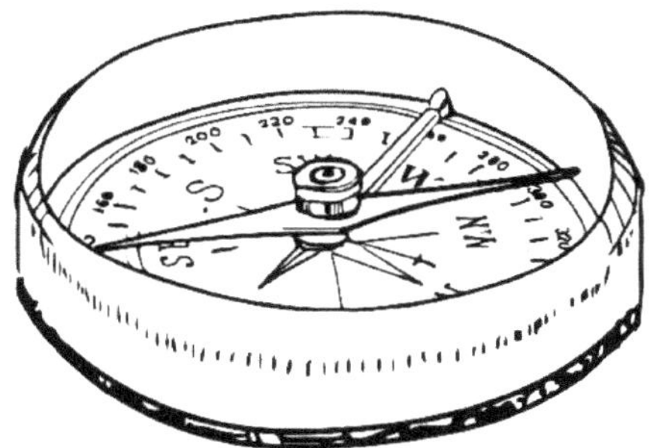

### ADVENTURE 1

- **You do not know what the change is to be,**
- **You have no internal change resources,**
- **You do have budget.**

Given where you are you may want to work with a more emergent change methodology. Appreciative Inquiry will be a good one for you as will Lean Change, as the feedback cycles can help you shape what the ultimate change vision is.

### ADVENTURE 2

- **You do know what the change is to be,**
- **You have no internal change resources,**
- **You do have budget.**

If you're recruiting resources, then you probably want to understand what methodologies influence them. If they can't talk to any methodology – or are not able to map out for you their (semi) structured approach to change – proceed with caution. In saying this, I don't want to imply that all change should be structured, far from it. There needs to be room for emergent change and synchronicity! However, someone who is not cognizant of the general stages of their logic may prove challenging from a success standpoint.

### ADVENTURE 3

- **You do know what the change is to be,**
- **You have internal change resources,**
- **You do have budget.**

In this instance, you may already have a preferred methodology within your organization, either bespoke or commercial. It's probably worth having a chat with your resources about how they have used the methodology successfully in the past, and ask them about where they think there are limitations. This will be a very insightful discussion.

### ADVENTURE 4

- **You may or may not know what the change is to be,**
- **You have internal change resources,**
- **You do have budget.**

I'm going to say in this situation, get yourself accredited in a commercial methodology quick smart. You're going to have a lot to think about and at least you will have a recipe to follow.

So, this concludes Part 1: Shaping up – the decisions you need to make. You are now able to have a considered conversation about your approach to change, who will do what, how you will define success, and what methodology you will make. Bravo! Being able to have this conversation should put you in a much more confident position than you were at the beginning, and I'm hoping you are feeling a bit more empowered to tackle Part 2, Moving Forward with Your Change. In this next section of the book we will look at how you build change capability within your business unit or organization, and ensure you are change ready. We'll look at change communication, and change leadership.

PART II

# Moving forward

Congratulations, you're up to date on the core concepts and the type of decisions you will need to make to lead or introduce your change effectively. In Part 2 we address the five pillars of your successful change initiative – change capability, change readiness, change resistance and stakeholder engagement, change communication, and change leadership.

# 7 Only the most capable

You'll recall in Chapter 5 I suggested that one of the markers of a successful change program is one that builds change capability in the rest of the organization.

A question that's core to many large corporates these days is *how* to build change capability. It's a great question – and one that when you unpack it, reveals many perspectives.

The value of organizational capabilities and the use of the word as corporate jargon rose to prominence with the strategic management researchers in the 2000s and subsequently was popularised by strategy consultants. Global strategy consulting firm McKinsey and Co defines organizational capabilities rather broadly as 'anything an organization does well that drives meaningful business results'.

Within the Resource Based View of the firm, a staple in the Strategic Management tool kit, academics Barney (1991) and Wernefelt (1984) recognised that organizational capabilities are a major source for the generation and development of sustainable competitive advantage. This view suggests that while many companies can copy or imitate products and services, organizational capabilities are more difficult to copy, and therefore provide a competitive edge. It's not that far of a stretch to see why change management as an organizational capability has risen in popularity. A company that is adept at managing change remains agile and can continuously generate sustainable competitive advantage.

The term capability is often used interchangeably with competence, but I tend to think in the context of organizational change it's broader than simply skill-sets. For me it comes down to answering a simple series of questions:

- What does it take for the organization to be highly capable of change?
- What does it take for our managers to be highly capable of change?
- What does it take for our people to be highly capable of change?

### 6 ELEMENTS OF A CHANGE CAPABLE ORGANIZATION

Change capability then looks something like the following:

1. An organizing structure for change management – this might be a governance model, a centre of excellence, or a centralised portfolio or internal consultancy.
2. Change management as a central construct in the learning and development systems (induction, internal courses, mentoring).
3. Change management as a central construct in the human resources systems (recruiting, performance management, and recognition).
4. Change as a cultural imprint within the leadership – lived values of innovation, agility, and of course, people.
5. Common supporting toolkits, frameworks, processes and templates that enable people to carry out successful change.

6. A multi-level framework that distinguishes between levels of capability (beginner, junior, novice, intermediate, senior / master).

## TO BUY OR BUILD?

One of the big dilemmas in building change capability is, do you try to do it internally, or do you need someone external to come in and do it? This will be factoring in to your resourcing decisions.

Some of the big names in the change management world (Gail Severini, Rich Bachelor, Garret Gitchell, Supriya Desai and Anai Spakowski) came together to discuss this challenge at the 2013 Association of Change Management Profession Global Conference. One of the panel members, Severini, published the following on her blog post, 'Optimizing internal and external change management (presentation and tip sheet)' as a summary of tips from the panel.

### For Organization Leaders:

- **The inclusion of externals *always* changes team dynamics. Be as explicit as possible about purpose and roles to both internals and externals (e.g. augmentation is very different from coaching).**
- **Treat your consultants and advisors as partners.**
- **Be explicit about skills transfer. Agree on who will be developed, how (e.g. training only? Observation? Coaching? How much and by whom?), and how achievement will be evaluated (e.g. what are demonstrable behaviours that prove capability?).**
- **Require that both internal and external Change Management practitioners collaborate effectively (thoroughly and in a timely**

manner), require individuals to work in person (or on video/phone) as much as feasible, and watch for symptoms (or lack thereof).

- Do proper onboarding for both. Less onboarding for externals will diminish their effectiveness.

For Internals:

- Remember: the success of an external is tied to the organization's success. They're there to help.
- Don't assume consultants know more - or that they think they do. They have specific knowledge that should be paired with your specific insights for optimal value.
- To avoid costly confusion, ask questions and don't assume—especially about roles.
- Provide feedback to externals - let them know what is and is not working.
- Build relationships with externals and seek their support in developing your capabilities.
- Be aware of how you feel - fear, anxiety, etc. - about the presence of external practitioners and how those feelings impact your interactions (positively or negatively).

For Externals:

- Be clear about your role and clients' expectations of you (e.g. do it for them, with them or teach them how).
- Meet clients where they are: be aware of their CM maturity.
- Invest in building relationships with internals - share information and resources, help sharpen their influencing skills, or coach them to see broader contexts, etc.

- **Be humble – no one feels safe when made to feel inferior.**
- **Remember that additional business will come if you deliver effectively on the current work, not if you manipulate events to impress leaders.**

Thinking about your organization – how does that fit for you? How would you rate yourself in terms of change capability? Your evaluation of change capability determines your change maturity. Change maturity is a way of identifying how mature your organization is with regards to instigating, managing and sustaining change.

## CHANGE MATURITY

The Change Management Institute have an impressive model of change maturity developed with the Carbon Consulting Group that is useful to think about in terms of your own organization.

It starts with five levels of change maturity – initial, repeatable, defined, managed, and optimised. These are described across three domains – project change (the initiators of most change), business readiness (the receiving end of change) and the strategic domain (what is driving the change).

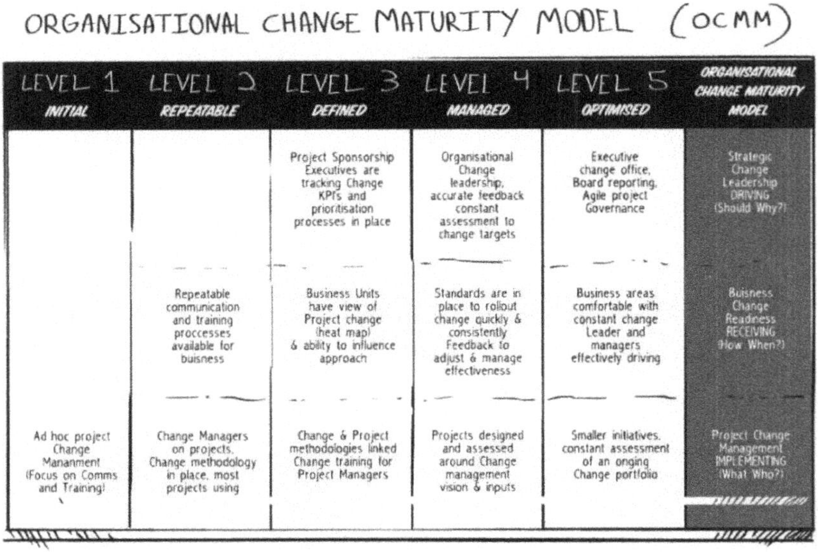

ORGANISATIONAL CHANGE MATURITY MODEL (OCMM)

| LEVEL 1 INITIAL | LEVEL 2 REPEATABLE | LEVEL 3 DEFINED | LEVEL 4 MANAGED | LEVEL 5 OPTIMISED | ORGANISATIONAL CHANGE MATURITY MODEL |
|---|---|---|---|---|---|
| | | Project Sponsorship Executives are tracking Change KPI's and prioritisation processes in place | Organisational Change leadership, accurate feedback constant assessment to change targets | Executive change office, Board reporting, Agile project Governance | Strategic Change Leadership DRIVING (Should Why?) |
| | Repeatable communication and training proccesses available for buisness | Business Units have view of Project change (heat map) & ability to influence approach | Standards are in place to rollout change quickly & consistently Feedback to adjust & manage effectiveness | Business areas comfortable with constant change Leader and managers effectively driving | Buisness Change Readiness RECEIVING (How When?) |
| Ad hoc project Change Mananment (Focus on Comms and Training) | Change Managers on projects. Change methodology in place, most projects using | Change & Project methodologies linked Change training for Project Managers | Projects designed and assessed around Change management vision & inputs | Smaller initiatives, constant assessment of an onging Change portfolio | Project Change Management IMPLEMENTING (What Who?) |

**Diagram 1.0: CMI OCCM Change Maturity Model**

Source: Carbon Group Consulting Pty Ltd Version 2.0 at **http://www.change-management-institute.com** (CMI White Paper, Change Agility, February 2012).

In my experience, most organizations sit at Levels 1 and 2. The large corporates are often at Level 3 and Level 4, but surprisingly, there are many who are not. I can't say I've seen any at Level 5. Why is this important to you? First, this may not be the only change initiative that you take accountability for. You may get away with Level 1 for this one, but it's worth thinking about how you contribute to developing change maturity across the business.

The second reason why you as an instigator and leader of change needs to think about change capability is, if you only consider the change management impacts of your own specific project (e.g.,

Level 1) AND NOT the broader business NOR align to the strategic changes going on, you can introduce a whole lot of noise into your work. It creates change fatigue for your stakeholders. You're talking about your change to people, other business leaders are talking about their change, the executive team is talking about change – and it all gets a bit loud and shouty!

If you can align your project change with the business change focus and the broader organizational change imperatives, you can get traction on your change. You're not competing with other initiatives – rather you're leveraging the momentum of other change around you. When you raise the change maturity of the business, you put change at the core of the culture and in doing this, you start to play in the exciting space of organizational agility.

One of the earlier points I raised as evidence of change capability was change as a cultural imprint within the leadership – lived values of innovation, agility, and of course, people.

Adaptability, flexibility, resilience and agility can all be considered attributes of change capability. *But who owns the development of these attributes?*

## WHO BUILDS CHANGE CAPABILITY?

It's a tricky one. In some organizations, it occurs slowly by osmosis when a new leader comes in and sets new cultural expectations. In other organizations, it belongs to the Human Resources / Human Capital / People function.

It might also belong to the Organizational Development team if you have one.

But, you know what? Dear manager, it most definitely belongs to you. All that you can do to develop your people's resilience, flexibility and adaptability serves you well when it comes to building change capability and ability to manage continuous change. Don't wait for someone else in the organization to own it.

Just do it.

### HOW IS CHANGE CAPABILITY BUILT?

There are several things that you as the manager can do to build change capability:

- When you work with your team ensure that you highlight and amplify moments of genuine optimism – challenge the negative talk you hear. It can be difficult to achieve balance between discouraging negative talk, and giving your team a safe space to speak honestly and frankly about their concerns.
- Focus on a strength based leadership style; when people are more aware of their strengths and know, they are appreciated, they're more resilient.
- Encourage open conversations about flexibility – flexible roles, flexible processes, see what you can let go of and role model flexibility for your people.
- When people talk to you about their fears, ask them to also note the opportunities. Sometimes people need help in achieving balance.
- Encourage your team to invest in their career development proactively.

- Have a monthly lunch where you have a presentation or discuss emerging trends.
- Always celebrate successes and achievements.
- Ensure that goal setting and review of goals is maintained during periods of change and also accommodate the new context of performance. Perhaps the goals need to be adjusted or there are new goals to include.
- Introduce your team to Stephen Covey's circles of control, influence and concern as a way to make sense of their reactions to things (see my must reads in Chapter 14 – from his book 'The 7 Habits of Highly Effective People')
- And finally, embrace and role model vulnerability. Stay open to sharing how *you* are experiencing the change.

This list provides you with ways of building change capability through bolstering resilience. The next list shares how to build change capability by building knowledge on corporate memory. There are other initiatives in the organization you may wish to sponsor or initiate to create change capability:

- Build 'WOL circles' – Chapter 13 will tell you more about these, but essentially, they are small groups where people work out loud on their changes, and are quite transparent about what they know and what they don't know.
- Create or sponsor a change management community of practice within your business that either meets in person or online, for example, in a yammer / LinkedIn or Facebook group.

- Initiate lean-in circles – ala the Sheryl Sandberg model. For more on Sandberg's model go to leanincircles.com
- Sponsor guest speakers with specialised knowledge to talk at team meetings or roadshows.
- Fund a corporate library of change resources.
- Back the business case for change management development via courses.
- Sponsor time out to attend Mass Open Online Courses (MOOCs) on change. For more help in who are running MOOCs go to http:// MOOC-List.com

**If not you then who and when?**

One thing to consider is that if you do not proactively build change capability and change maturity, you will have it forced upon you. This may be because of the latest trends and developments in technology systems. If your change initiative involves introducing cloud based systems, it may well be that you will be fast tracked into change capability before you know it. Let me explain… It's a little bit chicken and egg.

Many organizations are moving to Software as a System based technology solutions where data are stored in the 'cloud', and the organization is on the same platform as many other organizations. And it's had me wondering, does the uptake of cloud-based systems change drive a continuous change culture? Or do you need to have a culture of continuous change to see the true benefits of cloud-based systems?

I first encountered this curious chicken and egg when working on a global Workday implementation. Workday is a SaaS based HR Information Service. From a change management perspective, SaaS implementations are very interesting. One of the organizational benefits of going to the cloud is that they are often much cheaper than 'on premise' implementation of software, hardware and licensing (e.g., SAP, Oracle). You effectively lease a software system, and it is the same version that all their other customers use. This means you are unable to customise to varying business needs. (That would reduce the economic benefit for the vendor and increase the costs to the organization).

It's effectively 'one-way, same-way' and you put your trust in the vendor to be at the cutting edge of the discipline, so you are not one-way, same-waying into backwards business practice. You can configure for legislative variations, but with every configuration, you need to weigh the cost / benefit ratio. More configurations mean more maintenance and bigger system admin teams.

So, whereas traditionally, and not to jump too far ahead in this book, good change management means engaging with all the business stakeholders to understand their wants and needs, and addressing many of these as possible, traditional change consultation with cloud-based change can be problematic. You should manage expectations very carefully, lest the stakeholder assumes they will see a solutions design document that reflects their business requirements before you move into production of the system.

It means that for many of the organizations that do this, the change challenge is to 'harmonize' processes – so take 30 different processes, and make them one in order to fit with the SaaS process. For stakeholders, this raises big conversations of acceptable loss. To gain the benefits of real time data, insights, time savings and efficiency, some will have to give up local ways of doing things that they are very attached to. Whether we look at change optimistically as a 'change slinky' where we collectively cycle upwards through learning and change episodes (see Chapter 14 on the big debates) or the conventional change lifecycle where we take people through the valley of despair and back out again to the intended benefits, there is big work to be done.

Here's where the need for change capability and a change mature organization becomes apparent. There's an interesting change opportunity / challenge that happens after you launch your change. Cloud based vendors push major changes to the system on a cyclical basis (e.g., every three months, six months, etc.). And while you'll have notice of it and can test it before it's live in your system, you have limited ability to say no to it. Think about every time LinkedIn or Facebook push a change to you? In leading or sponsoring this change, you will need to think about your change governance model – how do you manage the continuous changes pushed through from the vendor.

It strikes me as a tremendous opportunity to build a culture of continuous change, agility and learning. In organizations where this type of culture is not apparent – could it be that in working through how you manage future releases of SaaS software, you also design for sustainability? Or is it in organizations that don't have a culture of continuous change, agility and learning that cloud-based releases become a painful process of scrambling to learn, adapt, communicate and deal with as you would any system change release?

It might be time to revisit the CMI Change Maturity model presented earlier and initiate some conversations with leadership on how you get to Level 4 before you end up immersed in some very difficult technology and digital transformations driven by SaaS platforms.

## CONVERSATION STARTERS

**Some of the conversations you might want to have right now are:**

- In considering the Change Management Maturity Model where would we describe our organization?
- How flexible, agile and adaptable would we describe our people?
- How might we improve the change capability – what is realistic over what time frame?
- If SaaS based change, how will we approach the change governance of continuous change?

## IMPLICATIONS FOR YOUR CHOICE IN ADVENTURE

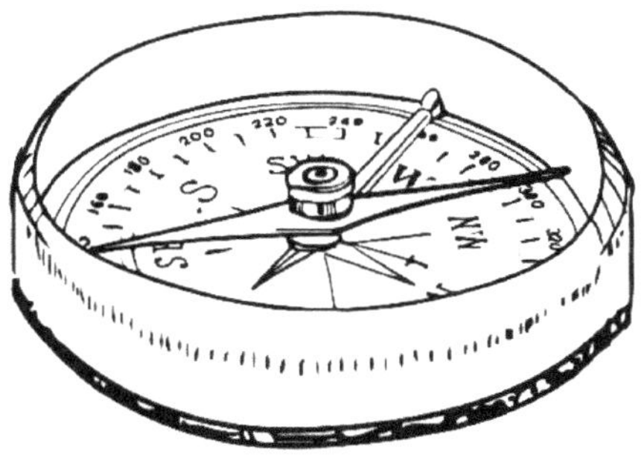

### ADVENTURE 1

- **You do not know what the change is to be,**
- **You have no internal change resources,**
- **You do have budget.**

An assessment of your organizational change capability will be very important in designing what your change will be and how you introduce it. You may end up moderating your ambition if the change maturity assessment reveals that you're not ready for the change.

### ADVENTURE 2

- **You do know what the change is to be,**
- **You have no internal change resources,**
- **You do have budget.**

You're most likely bringing in external change resources. You want to have explicit conversations about transfer of knowledge and capability, otherwise you might see a success spike which occurs during the change implementation period when the resource is there, but declines when they leave the organization.

### ADVENTURE 3

- **You do know what the change is to be,**
- **You have internal change resources,**
- **You do have budget.**

Those on Adventure 3 have a higher-level change maturity and change capability than other adventurers by virtue of the fact that there is already a recognised need for change management in the creation of change resources. It will be important to work with your change resources to understand what the change radar looks like – what else is landing at the same time as you wish to so that you're not overloading the business with change. This may not be a problem if you have a very high change maturity though; this might be a very agile organization.

## ADVENTURE 4

- **You may or may not know what the change is to be,**
- **You have no internal change resources,**
- **You have no budget to hire anyone.**

I think we can safely assume that you are in an organization with relatively low change maturity and change capability. It doesn't have to stay this way; it may be that with the content in this chapter you can be at the vanguard of innovation and change in your organization. Don't be overwhelmed by it – you are building from scratch so now is the time to consider these foundation elements.

In the next chapter, we address change readiness. This is the stage that's critical in assessing when you can go live, and what you need to do to give yourself the best opportunity for successful change.

# 8 Ready or not, here I come...

Often related to an understanding of change capability is the concept of change readiness. You need to be thinking about how ready your organization is for change. Change readiness is another buzzword in the change world which basically assesses 'Will they (the people) change?' and 'Can they (the people) change?'

## CHANGE READINESS DEFINED

Change readiness was initially defined as 'the cognitive precursor to the behaviours of either resistance to, or support for a change effort' (Armenakis, Harris and Mossholder, 1993, p. 681). It was seen as largely as attitudinal, how people thought and felt about change. Today, the construct, at least at a practical level, has come to include considerations of organizational support as well, so not just 'will they', but also 'can they' (e.g., do they have the skills, knowledge, resources, training, infrastructure, assets). You can have all the will in the world and be emotionally and intellectually supportive of change, but without the resources and capability you are simply not change ready.

Research in the field uniformly points to a lack of multi-level attention to change readiness. Change readiness occurs at an organizational level, a group level and an individual level. I've found that in practice, while the organizational and group levels are often addressed, we see individual readiness to change neglected. To be fair, it can be very resource intensive – an intervention at a team level is much simpler than doing twenty individual interventions.

That said, I prefer to focus on change readiness rather than resistance. In some ways, it presents as a way to do the Lewinian force field analysis. Kurt Lewin is one of the founding fathers of change management and in his early work, he established that there were forces for change and forces against change – you are change ready when the forces for change are greater than the forces against change. I think that when you focus on change resistance that's often all you will see ('when your only tool is a hammer, everything looks like a nail'). And for a whole host of reasons which I will explain in the next chapter, I think change resistance has limited use to us when we are implementing workplace change. However, by focusing on change readiness and you shift the energy a little bit, it's a more constructive focus.

## YOU NEED TO MEASURE

In practice, you want to use change readiness as a state that is measured at a point in time. It's measured in several ways – full blown quantitative surveys, pulse polls (short series of questions to take the pulse of the change), pulse checks – (checking in with change networks as representative of the audience), focus groups, and manager assessments. Done well, this data provides you with information on how, where and when to intervene to improve the likelihood of success when the change goes live.

In about half of my change engagements the change readiness assessment was aborted, the reasons being:

- The organization has survey fatigue.
- There is no time or resources to do anything about the results.

- Leadership is uncomfortable with hearing if the audience is not ready.

This is a real shame. Because one of the hidden benefits of a change readiness assessment is that it's a form of engagement and opportunity to reinforce the key messages of the change.

## CHANGE READINESS APPLIED

In a recent project where there was resourcing, time, and political understanding of the importance of the activity, we developed an audit tool to assess the business unit before go-live. The tool listed a series of practices which were known to either hinder or help the change once implemented with a 5-point scale. It provided a scoring scale, (e.g., what your score means, and a contact point to return the audit). The business unit leaders were asked to rate their business unit on these practices.

To be honest, I expected the business unit leaders to inflate the responses – I didn't mind that. Even if they were scoring themselves a 5 (when the real practice was lower), by thinking about the question they were being reminded of the key practices that needed to occur and saying to themselves, 'Oh boy, we are going to need to change this!' But the answers came in quite honestly and realistically. This enabled us to consolidate the results by business unit, and provided the change leaders with a focus on where to intervene with coaching / workshops / discussions on the changes to occur.

In other projects, I have been able to include a communication audit with the activity and provide critical information on the understanding of the key messages and what has missed the mark, so it's not an activity to be done in isolation. In crafting the change readiness activity, make sure you review what you want to do with other key stakeholders. You may be able to get more bang for your buck.

If you revisit Chapter 5 on what your success metrics are, you should be able to retro-fit your readiness measures. Are your teams and employees ready to achieve success in the areas that are important to you? What are the precursors to achieving these outcomes? These becomes your markers of change readiness.

For other examples, it's worth having a look at Heather Stagl's templates in her 'Influence Change at Work Tool Kit' at http://www.enclaria.com. We have a change chat with Heather in the next chapter. The reason why I like these ones is that Heather addresses change readiness at four levels:

1. Are individuals ready for change?
2. Is the organization ready for change?
3. Is the project ready for change?
4. And are you, as a change agent ready for change?

There's different elements for each of those four categories and it measures each of those four based on those different elements.

## CONVERSATION STARTERS

**Some of the conversations you might want to have right now are:**

- What does our intuition tell us about our organization's change readiness for this change?

- Is there a notable difference between the Will They, and the Can They?
- If an assessment comes back and shows low change readiness, do we have the resources to address it?

### IMPLICATIONS FOR YOUR CHOICE IN ADVENTURE

#### ADVENTURE 1

- **You do not know what the change is to be,**
- **You have no internal change resources,**
- **You do have budget.**

Like organizational change capability, a presumptive assessment of your organizational change readiness will be helpful in the design of your change. Ultimately, change capability is more important than change readiness. Without change capability, you are unlikely to shift the dial on change readiness.

#### ADVENTURE 2

- **You do know what the change is to be,**
- **You have no internal change resources,**

- **You do have budget.**

One of the thing to discuss with your change resources is when and how to assess change readiness. As you do have budget, you may be able to resource the assessment and interventions post assessment. Probably, one of the most important considerations in this discussion is the level of survey or assessment fatigue or availability of platforms to poll people.

### ADVENTURE 3

- **You do know what the change is to be,**
- **You have internal change resources,**
- **You do have budget.**

Have a chat with your internal resources about what they have done in the past to assess change readiness, and do they have formal milestones in a change process where they review change readiness. If they don't and haven't, perhaps show them this chapter and ask to them to come back to you with their recommendations.

### ADVENTURE 4

- **You may or may not know what the change is to be,**
- **You have no internal change resources,**
- **You have no budget to hire anyone.**

With no budget, and no resources, you're in a bit of a bind, but I think it's important you do at least one review of change readiness before you make the decision to go-live. You will most likely need to rely on qualitative feedback – ask your business unit leaders to lead a discussion on the topic and report back to you. If you have an Enterprise Social Network (ESN) like Yammer, maybe you could initiate a public discussion – as are we ready for this change?

In this chapter I flagged that I gave more credit to change readiness rather than change resistance, and I will explain more in the next chapter.

The next chapter addresses why change resistance is often a furphy – and why stakeholder engagement will be your friend in a successful change.

# 9 Resistance is futile

## (BUT FREAKING ANNOYING WHEN YOU EXPERIENCE IT)

In the last chapter I said that I don't tend to put much stock in focussing on change resistance. In this chapter I explain I why, but also offer you some things to think about when you experience 'change resistance' in your organization. Just because I don't focus on it doesn't mean that you won't experience it.

Historically (and frustratingly a lot of the time today), change resistance was / is seen as this immovable force needing to be overcome in order to achieve change success. Way back in 1979, Kotter and Schlesinger published 'Choosing Strategies for Change' in the Harvard Business Review. In it they proposed six strategies to manage resistance in order of difficulty.

1) Education and Communication
2) Participation and Involvement
3) Facilitation and Support
4) Negotiation and Agreement
5) Manipulation and Co-option
6) Implicit and Explicit coercion

As the change resistance force grows, you move down the list to use a tactic of greater strengths. In the article, they list the pros and cons of each approach and when it's best to use them. It's all pretty sensible stuff, but once the topic moves out of the text it all gets a little simplistic.

When managers hear objections to the change they want to implement there can be much hand-wringing about employees who are resistant to change. The call goes out to consultants who can assist with reducing or overcoming resistance to change.

And I really, *really*, think this is a very short-sighted view. More recently, change researchers (Piderit, 2000, Waddell and Sohal, 1998, Bovey and Hede, 2001) have recognised that change resistance is actually a far more nuanced and dynamic personal experience of change. What is seen as 'resistance' is multidimensional and often as not, a positive and constructive aspect of the change process. I'm with them. Here's why I get frustrated with a focus on change resistance as a negative thing and something to be 'overcome'.

### WHY FOCUSING ON CHANGE RESISTANCE IS NOT HELPFUL

1) Change resistance is multidimensional and there are so many emotions associated with a 'resistant view' it would take a team of organizational psychologists working full time to assist in working through it. I don't know about you, but I have rarely seen that resourcing.

2) The reactions associated with change resistance change from day-to-day and hour-to-hour. It is too dynamic to 'overcome'.

3) When people express resistance to change, they are actually engaging in the change. They are invested enough to consider it and respond. This is a good thing.

4) Resistance to me is feedback – as change agents and leaders of change you get the opportunity to respond to that feedback.

5) Often resistance is used as an excuse for poorly communicated or designed change. It's easier to blame the employees than reflect on the design of the change process.

6) Sometimes change resistance is an indicator of change fatigue. To 'overcome' change resistance in an environment of continuous change is fraught with danger. Consider those who are resistant as the canaries in the mineshaft.

## NEUROSCIENCE AND CHANGE RESISTANCE

There's also some interesting neuroscience behind not focusing on change resistance. One of the core aspects of motivation and goal achievement and brain function involves the 'Reticular Activating System' or RAS. The RAS is responsible for sifting through the millions of messages you get each day and making sense of them all. It's very efficient. Crudely put, when you focus on change resistance, your RAS seeks out examples of resistance and ignores the rest. That's just a little bit too risky for me.

For me, 'change resistance' is normal. We coach our managers to understand that it's normal to experience a performance dip after the implementation of a change that has some level of loss involved in it, and it's also normal to hear expressions of resistance.

Often, what we are hearing is:

- I don't know I have the skills for this.
- I don't think you have explained why very clearly.

- I really want this to happen but I don't want it to screw up.
- Show me proof this is going to work.
- Have you considered how we have failed at this before?

So, in the last chapter, I talked of the value in considering change readiness. For me this represents a more valuable aspect of change management. I recognise expressions of resistance as engaged stakeholders and work with them accordingly, and I accept that will be a continuous part of how employees make sense of change. But I put my focus on change readiness. This gives a much more targeted activity to do to move the business forward in their change goals. I tell my RAS to focus on change readiness and this draws out much more information and evidence that can be worked on in a positive and productive sense.

## THE FLIPSIDE: STAKEHOLDER ENGAGEMENT

That's all well and good, but you may still be wondering what I do with the resistance I see in front of me? OK, try this for size.

***'Change resistance is inversely proportional to the amount of stakeholder engagement that occurs.'***

Yep – every voicing of concern, anger, fear, sadness, frustration with your change is an invitation to start a conversation of sensemaking and possibility. Do that and those pesky resistant folks say, 'You're welcome'.

Not feeling confident in how to have that conversation? That's a different matter – try practicing conversation using the table below. Think through the potential responses to enable you to enter the conversation.

| | UNLIKELY | POSSIBLE | DEFINITELY | RESPONSE |
|---|---|---|---|---|
| This isn't the most important thing | | | | |
| I don't have time for this | | | | |
| I don't know what's going on | | | | |
| There's nothing in this for me | | | | |
| It isn't feasible | | | | |
| It's not my job | | | | |
| Nobody else is doing it | | | | |
| Why can't things stay the way they were? | | | | |
| This isn't a change for good | | | | |
| I don't believe in the basis for this change | | | | |

**Diagram 2.0: How to prepare for stakeholder engagement**

The more you engage with your stakeholders and borrow from Stephen Covey ('Seek first to understand, then be understood'), the less you need to deal with change resistance. Here's another template that you might find useful. You can adapt it easily. Brainstorm all the expressions of resistance that you think you will encounter and put them on the left. Run a probability assessment on likelihood of hearing them. Start with the ones most likely to be encountered and critically evaluate: is there merit in the expression? Why might it be valid? How can you engage someone with that position in a way that validates their concern?

## SURRENDER – AN ALTERNATIVE TO RESISTANCE…

And if you are feeling bold then you may like to consider thinking about resistance from an alternative perspective. That of 'surrender'.

Prior to publishing this book, I have been working through the concept of surrender in workplace change. My interest in the idea arose when I experienced 'stuckness', or perhaps 'resistance', when facing personal change because of a physical injury. Being able to surrender to the process was the point at which I moved from resistance into acceptance and changing how I lived, and therefore changing for the better. But it wasn't easy!

One of the popular change tools is the Conner Change Curve. In its original version, published in the Journal of Training and Development, 1982, it has eight stages with opportunities to keep increasing in organizational support, or points where people may drop out (contact – awareness – understanding – positive perception – experimentation – adoption – institutionalization – internalization).

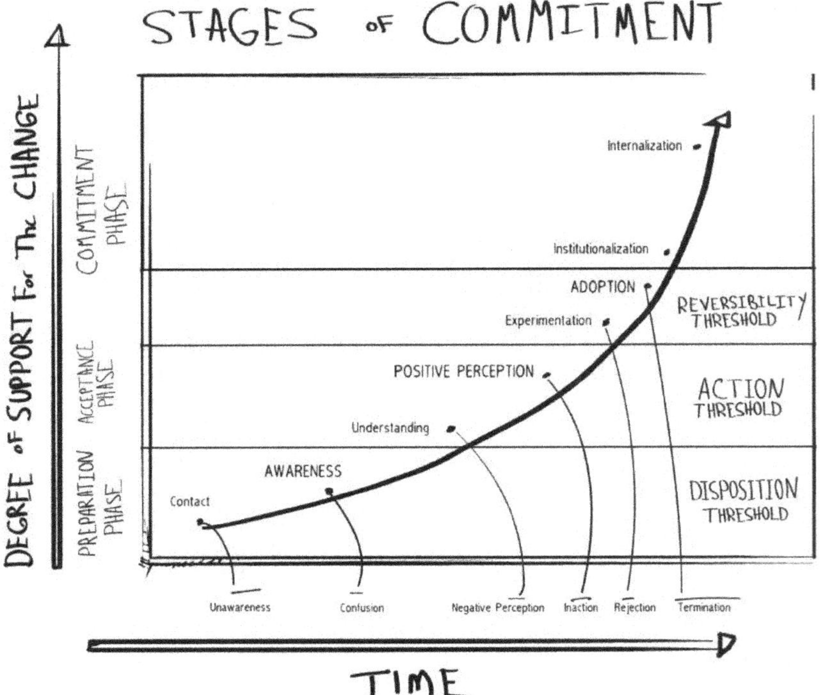


**Diagram 3.0: The Eight Stages of Building Commitment, Daryl Conner, www.connerpartners.com**

It has become truncated in many practitioners' tool kits to represent four stages – awareness, understanding, buy in and commitment.

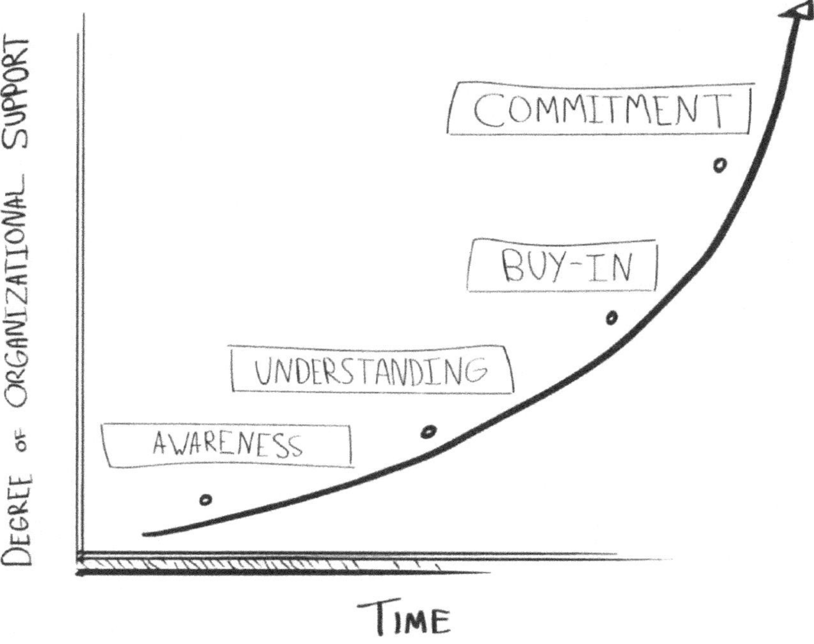


**Diagram 4.0: Conner's Commitment Curve adapted**

My own personal experience triggered some thinking about how Conner's change commitment curve might be missing a stage – a stage of Surrender. Initially, it takes a lot to consider surrender. Most of our definitions and popular references of surrender are negative and steeped in weakness or loss of control (captured in war, the surrendered wife, surrendering to a higher power). But on thinking about it more, I wondered if it wasn't something we could consider a strength – the ability to surrender, let go, and move with change.

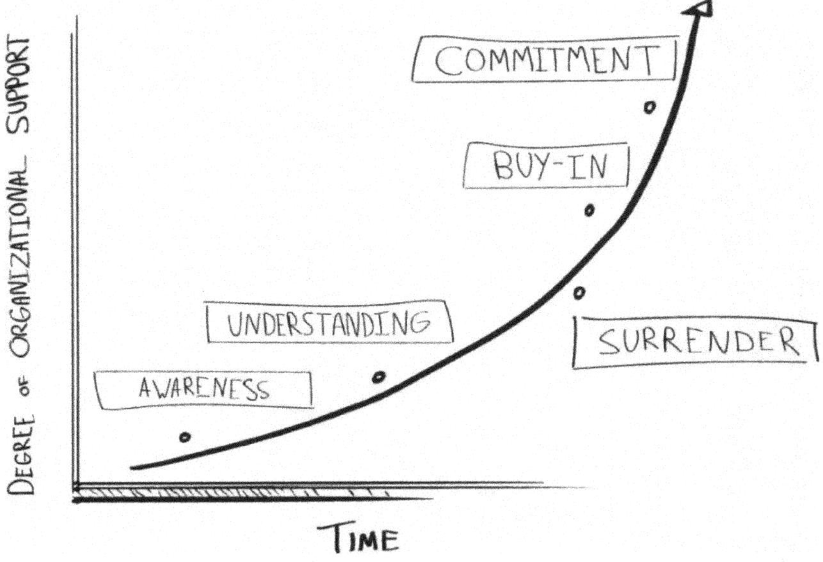


**Diagram 5.0: Commitment curve adapted for Surrender**

You will find with your change that it's relatively easy to take people through stages of contact, awareness and understanding – and yet it may not lead to positive perceptions and experimentation. That's why I am wondering if Conner's change curve could benefit from considering 'surrender' as a stage? Or as Caroline Kealey of Ingenium Communications describes it, 'the hinge' that moves people from head (contact / awareness / understanding) to heart (positive perception) and hands (experimentation). In thinking this through, I think 'surrender' as a way of managing change resistance is a three-part concept, that is steeped in past, present and future considerations.

## PART 1 IS ABOUT TRUST

Part one addresses the past and historical actions of leadership. For people to 'surrender' they need to be able to trust the leadership team. Only in this aspect it's not so much what can be done as who the change leader or leadership team is. Their character (s), their past behaviours, their current actions. Can the change leader(ship) be trusted? Do they speak with authenticity, transparency and honesty? Do their actions align with their words. I think 'trust' becomes a necessary pre-condition for surrender.

## PART 2 IS MINDFULNESS

Mindfulness is steeped in the present. People need to be mindful of the experience of change – the stress, the excitement, the fear, the anxiety that leads to them to get bound up in a psychic prison of 'what if' – amplifying concerns and thinking through the implications to the point where no action occurs (trying the change, practicing the new steps, behaving in new ways, exploring the new system). Moments of meditation, breathing, relaxing muscles that have tensed during the day assist the employee to experience the sensory aspect of change.

Whereas a lot of the commentary about corporate mindfulness programs is about employee health and well-being, what if there is an additional bonus? That organizations that encourage mindfulness, meditation, yoga and reflection in the workplace are just better at continuous change?

## PART 3 IS ABOUT FAITH

Faith addresses the future. Unless the employees have faith in the future state, it is unlikely they will surrender to 'buy-in'. And this becomes the role of the change practitioner and the change leader. Creating and communicating a vision that is believable, that resonates, that the employees can believe in. They may not be able to see it right now, but they have faith it will happen. They are willing to 'surrender' to change.

Are all three equal in weighting? Perhaps not. If you have low trust and faith, the need for mindfulness is higher (as the physical and psychological effects of the lack of trust and faith are higher). Strong mindfulness and strong faith in the future may offset a leader who is not trusted. Not ideal though. I'm not sure you get 'surrender' without all three. But I do know that Surrender is necessary to move to hands and heart, buy-in and commitment.

## CONVERSATION STARTERS

**Some of the conversations you might want to have right now are:**

- If you think about change resistance with your change – what are the potential reasons?
- How does the concept of surrender sound to you? The threepart recipe?
- If you were to increase the stakeholder engagement, where would you start? With who and for what reason?

## IMPLICATIONS FOR YOUR CHOICE IN ADVENTURE

### ADVENTURE 1

- **You do not know what the change is to be,**
- **You have no internal change resources,**
- **You do have budget.**

Ah, the excitement of a clean slate to work with. Okay, so forget about change resistance completely, and in designing what your change will be, make sure you have done a very thorough stakeholder identification activity and stakeholder engagement plan. This will set out who your stakeholders are, what their concerns are with the change and how you will address them.

### ADVENTURE 2

- **You do know what the change is to be,**
- **You have no internal change resources,**
- **You do have budget.**

If you have brought change resources in from outside, they will most likely want to start with a stakeholder identification process and be asking a lot of questions about the stakeholders' position on the change. This means that you are already addressing change resistance – either current or potential. You're in good hands. Keep the focus on frequent engagement and looking at how to ensure the organization is ready for change.

### ADVENTURE 3

- **You do know what the change is to be,**
- **You have internal change resources,**
- **You do have budget.**

Okay, the tricky bit with internal resources is sometimes they are so used to their internal stakeholders they have blinkers on about what the sources of change resistance are. Conversely, they often have a deep understanding of the business concerns. Your job here will be to make it safe enough for them to tell you about the 'elephant' in the room, the real reason why people may be uncomfortable with the change, and to push them to take a fresh look at their stakeholders.

### ADVENTURE 4

- **You may or may not know what the change is to be,**
- **You have no internal change resources,**
- **You have no budget to hire anyone.**

This will be an interesting space for you to work in, as good stakeholder engagement is time intensive and you will most likely be tempted to just focus on rolling out this change. All I can offer you now is assurance that the more time you put into stakeholder engagement listening to concerns, and responding to these concerns, the better you will be when it comes to launching this change.

The next chapter is a big one, it's on change communication. But I promise you, it is sooo important to your change. Take your time, it's worth going through it all.

## CONVERSATION OF CHANGE WITH HEATHER STAGL, FOUNDER, ENCLARIA LLC

**Dr. Jen:** Heather, can you tell me, how do you define change resistance?

**Heather:** Sure. The dictionary definition of resistance is any force that slows down or prevents motion. It's just a scientific term that you can find in physics and electricity and all kinds of things. We've sort of adapted that in change because it feels like resistance is any force that slows down or prevents change. But really, when it comes down to it, it's more like resistance means that other people aren't changing with the enthusiasm that I expect them to have. They're not engaged as much as I want them to be and that's when we realized that people might be resisting change. It's really in the eye of the beholder. That change resistance doesn't really happen unless we expect something different from what's happening.

**Dr. Jen:** So, change your expectations?

**Heather:** Things that we call change resistance, when we're going through change, we think it's a perfectly normal thing to do. But when we're the ones that are trying…

**Dr. Jen:** The flipside there is if we change our expectations of what will occur, we won't see resistance.

**Heather:** Yeah, it would at least feel different.

**Dr. Jen:** Yeah. You've previously done a very successful TEDxTalk on resistance – I'm working on an assumption that since the Ted Talk on resistance, you're thinking about resistance has perhaps deepened or changed or gone on different paths. Is that the case and where have you gone since the Ted Talk in thinking about resistance?

**Heather:** The overall philosophy hasn't really changed. It's still that idea that it's not something to overcome it's something to uncover. I dig into the eight sources of resistance. I can just list them quickly…

**Dr. Jen:** Please. Do that.

**Heather:**

1) One is valid concerns. 'This is just a bad idea' or 'It's going to affect me negatively, so I'm not going to like it'. That's the most obvious.
2) A lack of information.
3) Skills deficit.
4) Low motivation.
5) No power. They're not empowered to change even though we think we've empowered them.
6) Another one is fear.
7) Absence of trust.
8) and the last one is scarce resources. I don't have enough time. I don't have enough money and all those reasons.

When you go through those and put yourself in their shoes to identify which of them is a possibility, it helps you have empathy. When you understand what they're going through, then you can come up with solutions to actually help them go through the change.

**Dr. Jen:** When you've used those eight reasons for change resistance with managers that you work with in your client base, are there any of those that stand out as ones that they get straight away? Or some that they get challenged…don't want to accept?

**Heather:** They get quite a few right away, but 'the fear' that's where people assume that resistance comes from. The one that's hard for people to accept, especially leaders, is the 'no power' one. If someone that works for them feels like they're not empowered to change, then that's really on the leader. It's a matter of looking in the mirror to see what it is that they are doing that is disempowering people.

**Dr. Jen:** One of the prevailing views that is out there in the change world is that often that we shouldn't be focusing on change resistance at all, that we should be focusing on the positive or on change readiness, that when we focus on resistance we're effectively blaming the employee for the lack of progress. When perhaps it should be put back onto the manager in terms of 'How have you defined this change?', 'How have you designed the change?', 'How have you executed the change?' and questioning whether the answers to those questions is perhaps what is getting in the way of success. What's your view on that view? Are you a subscriber to that or…?

**Heather:** I can definitely see where people are coming from when they talk about focussing on readiness and not on resistance. One of the reasons that I like to talk about resistance is because, as change practitioners, that's where we come from, that's what we experienced. If we just focus on readiness and don't talk about the resistance that we are experiencing from other people, then we're ignoring our own feelings. We have to acknowledge that we're frustrated with people, but then recognize again that it's not something they're doing on purpose to you.

I really think looking at resistance is a gateway to empathy…

# 10 Change communication

For many managers and leaders in organizations, change communication is akin to the internal marketing of the change. There are some strong parallels, but I would resist the urge to ask your marketing department to help you out. You do need someone with strong experience in change communication to help you structure your communication strategy and plan. The similarities between change communication and internal marketing, however, are as follows:

- Addresses an act of consumption (product, service, message, new organizational practice).
- Starts with a comprehensive stakeholder analysis (who is the purchaser, the user, the audience we are addressing?).
- Is concerned with identifying influencers and engaging their participation.
- Uses multiple media / channels to introduce the new (product, service, message, organizational practice).
- Responds immediately to feedback that indicates difficulty in accepting the new product / process / service / practice.
- Engages the consumers / employees on a continuous basis to provide feedback back to the organization on product / service / process / structure redesign.
- Treats the consumers / employees as partners in the future of the organization and focuses on the relationship development and maintenance.

- Understands that focusing on control is a quick path to cynicism about the message content.
- Can go ridiculously pear-shaped regardless of the composition of the team delivering the campaign / programme and the preparation that has been done!
- Understands that small conversations are the key to successful adoption of the new idea / product / practice.

## CHANGE COMMUNICATION – MONOLOGIC, DIALOGIC AND THE BACKGROUND TALK

Let's explore the nuances of good change communication further.

Often change communication means Fact Sheets, FAQs, Roadshows and Manager Talking Points. *Good* change communication means timely information that's fed to the troops providing a consistent message and clarity in meaning. And if that's the worst we get out of change communication, then we're probably not doing so badly.

But I'm going to encourage you to consider a broader understanding of change communication. Change communication is more than just a tool to introduce the new system, structure or values. Change communication represents a mindset that sees organizational change as the result of a series of communicative events. The communication within the organization creates the change we need to make.

## MONOLOGUES AND DIALOGUES

Organizations can be considered as consisting of monologues or dialogues. Monologic change communication is identified as topdown, one-way, instrumental communication. When the change communication is monologic, we speak with the same voice, shared understanding, and the power lies with those who make the decisions about the change.

On the other hand, dialogic change communication is constructive in nature. Relationships matter, different perspectives matter, and power is shared among all within the organization. The front-line employee has as much voice as the CEO. The nature of dialogic communication is about creating new meaning, processes, or products out of the conversations.

As described above, both terms monologic and dialogic change communication suggest purposeful and deliberate uses of formal communicative action within organizational change. However, we can't forget the informal communication of change, or the conversations that go on in the background. This was a core finding from my PhD research into how change communication impacts employees' receptivity to change.

## INTRODUCING THE BACKGROUND TALK

Many conversations of change occur through the grapevine, by the water cooler, and within the corridor conversations. How employees individually make sense of change can dominate the formal narrative of change, and this sense-making produces a 'background talk of change'. The background talk can serve as a barometer of how receptive the employees are to the changes being introduced.

So, in answering the initial question, change communication includes monologic communication, dialogic communication, and the informal background conversations of change.

Of course, in considering a broader understanding of change communication, we add complexity to the change communicator's efforts. Let's face it, preparing FAQs and Talking points is so much easier. Reducing the complexity of change communication can be assisted by asking the question: 'What is the purpose of your communication?'

The simplest answer to this question comes from the age-old dialectic of change and stability. What do you want to do? Do you want to *create more change* with your communicative efforts? Or do you want to use communication to *create some stability* amongst the change program?

The use of Fact Sheets, FAQs, Roadshows and Manager Talking Points creates stability. In a time of uncertainty, these tools provide some information that can reassure, educate and clarify the details of what the employee is unsure of.

Managers seek to stabilise the organization by communicating vision and educating employees on the benefits of the intended change. It's reflected in speech, acts or written directives that suggest a one-way direction. This unilateral trajectory assumes a high degree of planned change, and that the manager or change communicator can control the message.

However, these are not the communication tools that assist you in creating further change. For this purpose, you have employee forums, Enterprise Social Networks (ESNs), and a communicative culture that values listening, and eschews hierarchical structures.

As discussed in an article in the Management Communication Quarterly (2000), authors Bokeno and Gantt suggest that dialogic communication is distinctly different from the usual patterns of management communication. It represents the ability to engage with genuine care and respect, to generate reflective discussion, and to speak authentically, and is seen to have positive impacts on innovation and organizational change.

This dialogic approach assumes that the managers and employees possess the requisite competences to carry the dialogue. It goes beyond strong interpersonal skills; it also means high emotional intelligence and managers willing to suppress status and ego. You need to be able to listen, to be empathetic, cognizant of differences to adopt communicative practice that creates further change.

## A MORE COMPREHENSIVE MODEL

However, the change and stability dialectic is a simple distinction, and not always one that captures the complexity of organizations that undergo change on a frequent and continuous basis. In their book, Organizational Communication in an Age of Globalization (2004), authors Cheney, Christensen, Zorn and Ganesh offer a more comprehensive and thoughtful model of change related communication.

The model indicates that the question 'What is the purpose of your change communication?' can be answered by four core change related activities: formulation, implementation, institutionalization, and dissemination.

1. **Formulation** – sometimes known as 'ideation', the phase where the organization generates an understanding of what the change outcome might be like. Note the inclusion of communicative acts such as experimentation. Rather than focus on planned change events, organizations that change continuously recognise the value of experimentation, adaptation and flexibility.
2. **Implementation** – this maps more closely with traditional understandings of change communication planning and implementation in that it is about how the message is introduced. But it also recognises the importance for change communicators to build networks of influencers, and that the process of implementation is more than a one-way process of message transfer. It is often a highly-contested space of resistance and negotiation.
3. **Institutionalization** – this phase recognises the importance of embedding the change initiatives, and the communicative acts that occur to celebrate and reinforce the changes.
4. **Dissemination** – the final phase recognises the value in publicising the change experience, but perhaps more importantly, sharing experiences. In an organization that changes continuously, it is important to process the learnings

from the previous change experience before embarking on the next.

These four phases operate within the social historical context. History matters. You cannot create a successful change communication experience in isolation from the history of the organization, and the social make-up of the employees.

At this point, take a moment to consider – do you think that the organization you work in is indicative of dialogic change communication or monologic change communication? I want to emphasise, one is not better than the other – it really does come down to your purpose and communication objectives.

If you can start by clarifying your purpose of communication during change, then you can start to map out what types of communication activities you will do and in what way.

## PITFALLS TO BE CAREFUL OF

Unfortunately, clarity of purpose is not enough with your change communication. There are still a myriad of pitfalls and booby traps ahead of you. Let's look at a few and how to avoid them.

### Authenticity

We ask a lot from leadership and managers in communicating change – we want them to be skilled communicators, able to engage multiple audiences in the same presentation or speech. We want them to be open and vulnerable and retain an ability to be seen as the leader. This challenge is enough to make most managers and leaders shrink away from the task… and just send an email. But here's the thing, dear manager: when you bring your whole self to your change communication and let your audience see you in all your facets, it creates multiple points of reference and all people can identify with you.

### Overly emotional

The next pitfall is the urge to create intense emotional messaging. If this messaging is focused on fear 'if we don't change, you lose your jobs', we risk the audience rejecting the messages (it's too awful to think of). A friend recently shared a horrific photo of animal cruelty on Facebook in an attempt to change people's behaviours with regards to buying leather. The photo was so horrific that within 18 hours I had resolved that it must be photoshopped and was angry at the animal cruelty activists who had generated it. That one backfired. The same thing happens in organizational change – you want to be thoughtful about tempering the mix of emotion and logic in your change communication.

### Identity

On the topic of rejection of message, another way is to base your argument around a value that the people do not identify with it. You may want to share change communication on the importance of the standardization of your practices – but perhaps your employees don't think of themselves as one-way, same-way kind of people. Instead, they perceive themselves as entrepreneurial and innovative folk. Your challenge is to find a higher order principle or value – one that unites all your people, and nobody can disagree with.

### To brand or not to brand

One of the most vexing decisions to make is, do you give your change project a 'name', or brand the change project? I lean on the side of 'no', just call it what it is. This is mainly because our audience or the employees get so exhausted by all the cute / twee / inspirational branded projects and trying to remember 'Ulysses, right – what's that one about again?', or they end up being very clever and coming up with alternative and cynical interpretations of change initiative names. It can be more informative and educational to simply call it what it is in as few words as possible. Make sure you think very clearly about the implications of acronyms as well. Project Information Standardization and Simplification doesn't bode so well when the employees get hold of it :-/

This also goes for the use of images – I swear, if I see one more image of the caterpillar becoming a butterfly for a transformation project (think about it, butterflies only live for one day) or the goldfish jumping to the other bowl (goldfish are not known for their brain size), I will lose it! If you're going to use images to communicate a representation of your change, proceed with thoughtful caution, rather than relying on a commercial image provider's option under 'change or transformation'.

### Over-communicating

There's ample warning in the change management literature of the potential disaster that's 'under-communication'. Best-selling authors Rosabeth Moss Kanter and John Kotter both note the criticality of communication to the success of organizational change. Poor communication of change is repeatedly cited as a core driver of change cynicism, apathy, anxiety and uncertainty based stress. When a change communication vacuum occurs, it's inevitably filled with rumour, gossip and misinformation. It's human nature to 'fill the gaps'.

But we hear little of the perils of 'over-communicating'. While many say, you can't over-communicate during change, I argue that you can. Over-communicating can also create anxiety, frustration, and cynicism. The negative effects of overcommunication result when:

- Management pushes a line that does not resonate with the employees (spin).
- The project team has neglected the awareness and understanding phase of change and have jumped straight to trying to sell messages to gain commitment (delivering the message 'here's why you must love this change', without introducing the change first).
- The timing of the communication is misaligned with the tempo of the change (bi- weekly huddles with nothing to say).
- The channels used aren't the preferred channels of the employees (ten daily emails could be replaced by one serious conversation).
- The source of the change communication is not well respected (blah, blah, he's talking again…).
- There are so many competing messages about various change projects they all blur into one big transformational white noise!

So how do you manage the Goldilocks version of change communication? Where what you deliver is 'just right'? It's harder than it looks, and this is where change people with communication expertise are well worth the investment. Some of the things to look out for are:

- A change communication strategy that is developed after research has been conducted on the change audiences – what their communicative preferences are (source, frequency, channels, jargon and language).
- An understanding of the communicative climate – what is acceptable and also what is taboo.
- An understanding of the balance between dialogue and topdown messaging.
- A communications plan tailored to the different stages of change commitment.
- The change communication plan has been reviewed and approved by the people you want to communicate to and with (not the project team / managers).
- A communication calendar which maps the various messaging from all the various initiatives and provides opportunity to 'cluster' the messages for simplicity's sake.

### But what of social media?

One of the opportunities for change programs now is social media. This is particularly so if you have customers or clients as one of your change targets, but also applicable to those whose change only affects the internal audiences. If there is a chance that your change will be discussed publicly on social channels, then you need to include your companies' social media team on briefings so they know how to respond and when to escalate. Do you remember how once upon a time people used to hear about their factory closing down on the radio? It's now twitter…

I think that your change communication people can take their lead from content curators in the social media space. One of the common challenges in organizations is that communicating the changes to all the identified stakeholders can be very difficult. They all use varying custom communications outlets; this can require a fragmented approach. Of course, this usually assumes a monologist approach – that you are communicating *to* an audience, not *with* an audience.

The alternative perspective of change communication in social media involves the generation of a content strategy. Making the information about the changes easily searchable, shareable, categorised, and findable. Potentially providing a daily or weekly digest, which makes it easy for all the stakeholders to find what they would like. If the underlying organizational systems support and promote multimedia content, then that shouldn't be too difficult.

The first steps include determining what to curate – what content currently exists, and what would be easy to generate around the change to be implemented? What are the sources that could be used? For example, YouTube, newsletter, intranet, SharePoint, industry articles, online news, company website, employee blogs.

Depending on how large and complex the organization is, the role of content curator in change may need to be an enterprise role, one that has oversight of all the changes coming through so that the organizing taxonomy makes sense. An employee receiving 12 different aggregation emails will be just as overloaded as the employee receiving the fragmented yet tailored pieces of information.

Social content expert Rohit Bhargava provides five models to consider in social marketing for content curation and I think you can apply them to change management.

1. Aggregation – curating the most relevant information about a particular change in a single location.
2. Distillation – pulling out the most simple and important messages within the change agenda.
3. Elevation – curating by identifying a larger trend or insights from smaller daily musings (e.g., the 'small wins and snowball' approach of change).
4. Mashups – unique, curated juxtapositions where content is merged to create a new point of view (a fabulous way of embedding culture change and supporting behaviour change or highlighting the gap analysis).
5. Chronology – bringing together historical information to show an evolving understanding (the change journey?).

So, there you have it. A lot to digest, but incredibly important for you to do so.

## CONVERSATION STARTERS

**Some of the conversations you might want to have right now are:**

- Some of the conversations you might want to have right now are:
- When we think about the best change communication we have experienced, what comes to mind?
- When change communication has not worked well, why was it?
- What are the communication objectives of this initiative?
- What do we think of the idea of curating content for this change – how could we use Bhargava's model?

### IMPLICATION FOR YOUR CHOICE IN ADVENTURE

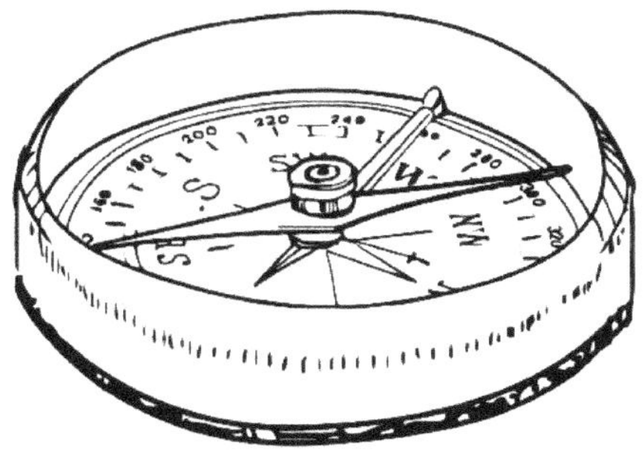

## ADVENTURE 1

- **You do not know what the change is to be,**
- **You have no internal change resources,**
- **You do have budget.**

Initially, a formal monologic change communication program isn't as important as defining your change, and ultimately it will be through dialogic change communication that you can achieve this purpose. Make sure you look at the options for co-creation – including people in conversation about what the issues are and the potential approaches. Through this strategy, you can start to test key messages and identify your audiences.

### ADVENTURE 2

- **You do not know what the change is to be,**
- **You have no internal change resources,**
- **You do have budget.**

This chapter will be helpful for you to review with your change communication resource. You don't need to develop a change communication plan or strategy, that's their job. But they do need to have considered the concepts and observations covered in this chapter.

### ADVENTURE 3

- **You do know what the change is to be,**
- **You have internal change resources,**
- **You do have budget.**

Again, this chapter will be useful to talk to your internal resources with. Encourage them to a 'change communication lessons learned' and identify the pitfalls they've seen in your organization. Ask them 'What is the change communication campaign you would have wanted to implement, but weren't allowed to?' Their answers may surprise you.

### ADVENTURE 4

- **You may or may not know what the change is to be,**
- **You have no internal change resources,**
- **You have no budget to hire anyone.**

I'm hoping this chapter is useful to you in thinking through what the purpose of your change communication is and the varying ways you can approach it. You may struggle with execution, so I would encourage you to soak up the next chapter on Leadership and simply communicate with as much transparency and frequency as you can.

## CONVERSATION OF CHANGE WITH CAROLINE KEALEY, OWNER, INGENIUM COMMUNICATIONS

**Dr Jen:** First, I want to say 'Congratulations on the Gold Quill Excellence award' and not only that The Best of the Best! This is kind of the Holy Grail of what you can win with the International Association of Business Communications professionals. Tell us about that, what did you win for and what was that experience like?

**Caroline:** Thanks Jen! It was an extraordinary experience to work with such terrific clients, and really build a deep partnership together in helping drive transformation. That's what stands out for me – it was a unique collaboration in which we worked side by side with the clients over the period of a few years. The level of trust, mutual respect and shared goals was remarkable. We jointly won IABC's global Best of the Best Award for change communications for a project we delivered in partnership with the University of Ottawa's Facilities Team.

When you think of a University, you don't often think of the infrastructure and mechanics that it takes to actually run a campus – but in fact, it's like operating a small city. The Facilities team is made up of

175 employees, which includes tradespeople such as plumbers, electricians, carpenters as well as architects, planners and engineers.

The team was going through a major business transformation to modernize their operations. The goal was to increase client satisfaction and deliver maximum value to the University.

As you know, award programs like IABC's are all about metrics – and that's one of the things that stands out in our collaboration with the University of Ottawa's Facilities team. The organization took measurement seriously and so we were able to tie our transformation and change communication efforts to actual business metrics of performance such as the cost to operate buildings per square meter, overtime costs, lost work time due to injury and so on. Together we were able to document that the transformation initiative yielded an increase in productivity of $2.9 million Canadian.

We worked with the management group to develop a very participatory communications campaign as the centrepiece of the transformation initiative. The idea was to emphasize employee engagement and involve staff in shaping the future of their work. This was powerful, because many of these employees really work in the shadow of the University – they are what makes the campus function, and yet there's very little visibility to their work. The campaign was designed around the theme of We Power Ideas – the concept was to tap into the intrinsic sense of motivation and purpose of the employees, making the connection between their vital work and the University's mission. We developed graffiti posters, videos and designed several opportunities for informal conversations for employees to create shared meaning and contribute to shaping their path forward in an open and constructive fashion. It was, in effect, a classic example of using culture as the source for solutions rather than as the problem to be fixed.

**Dr Jen:** What, in your experience, particularly the last 15 years with your business, what do you think differentiates adequate change communication to high impact change communication?

**Caroline:** I would say that the big picture answer is that change communication really has to do with going beyond information dissemination and really getting at translation and creation of shared meaning. There is something much more experiential when you are dealing with change because there is no amount of information, there is certainly no email that going to save you in the face of a change dilemma. You really have to find a way to engage at the heart level on the emotive plane, so that then people are receiving information through that culture of emotion in a way that's conducive to where you are going. That process is much more conversational in nature, and frankly runs up squarely against the very traditional command and control approach to communication that is the default in many organizations today.

For example, one of the simplest and most powerful change communications activities we've used with our clients is to create regular, predictable opportunities for conversations. Often, we call these dialogue sessions. In the case of the University of Ottawa project, the change sponsor was the Executive Director of Facilities, Claudio Brun del Rel – a lovely man who was enormously respected by his team, but had little day-to-day contact with front-line employees working across the campus. So, we set up simple sessions we called 'Coffee with Claudio', where employees could meet at regular points on a monthly basis for informal conversations about the changes. I think part of the success here is the idea that there is a predictable, regular cycle to these sessions – so that if people have questions or become anxious, they know that an opportunity to have a safe space to talk about the change will be coming. Also, an important factor is that these sessions are unscripted and unplugged – it's not about PowerPoint, but rather just bouncing ideas, socializing new ways of thinking and working and connecting the dots. It's really a creative process of creating line of sight between the big picture strategic direction, and what that means on a day-to-day basis. For example in the case of Facilities, it might be a question like: 'we're now interested in delivering value to the University and I am electrician, what is it that you want me to do?' Fundamentally, people want to perform and contribute, but often the space between high level strategic direction and what that means for day-to-day work is unclear. Through dialogue and conversation, this line of sight can be animated and come to life through a co-creative process. This takes time – but it is critical to creating sustainable, meaningful change.

Change communication success doesn't take huge budgets, but it does take discipline, commitment and the courage to work in an open, iterative fashion in which sometimes executives don't have all the answers.

One of the most successful communications tactics we used with the Facilities team was a video showcasing the behind the scenes work of the team. It was professionally produced, but designed to be a bit fun, and play up the culture and the family spirit of the team. An important indicator of success for us was not only the employees' enthusiasm for participating in the video and then watching it, but them going a step further and creating off-shoot videos on their own. This idea of user-generated content is nirvana in communications and marketing – where the audience actually gets involved in spreading the message in an authentic way by getting involved in the creative process using their own ideas and their own voice. In this case, we had operations employees make videos like a fast-motion clip showing all the work that goes into setting up a gymnasium for exams. To me, that was a significant signal that we were tapping into something really important – in reaching that sense of intrinsic motivation and meaning in the team's work.

Of course, all this effort took a lot of time and sustained attention. But the truism in change communications is that you can have it fast, or you can have it with employee engagement… pick one of the two.

# 11 Leadership – a very short chapter

So, I signalled in Chapter 5 that many people perceive that change leadership is the most important element of executing successful change, more so than change communication. And I have empathy with that perspective as much as my world is ridiculously biased by the importance of change communication.

You can create the best change communication in the world, but if there is no change leadership, or the leaders of the organization are not demonstrably supporting and committed to the change, your words won't mean much. For, you see, a leader's actions are highly symbolic – and symbols and the sense we make of them always trump what is spoken and written.

But, to be frank, I'm a little bit stumped on what to write in this chapter. It could end up rather short. You either chose to lead change or you don't.

**It's a NIKE imperative – Just do it!**

There is much argument academically over whether leaders are born or made. I believe while some people inherently possess leadership traits, you can develop leadership traits and behaviours if you are willing. I've taught leadership subjects in postgrad – it has always felt like padding out the semester to me though. Yet, students often tell me it's the subject they enjoyed the most. So maybe the appetite to take up leadership positions is widespread.

And if you're in that group, hungry to show leadership, now is your chance.

So, here's what I know about change leadership from my experience in organizations, not the academic texts.

### CHANGE LEADERSHIP TAKES COURAGE AND BRAVERY

Often you have to hold the ground of a course of action in the face of very emotion fuelled and politically motivated opposition. You sometimes have to put forward an idea that will be threatening or uncomfortable. And it can feel scary, especially initially when there is not momentum for the change and when it's new and novel. It also can get very scary as you are ready to launch your change or in the days immediately after. Just make sure you revisit the chapter 5 on defining your success metrics. These should be able bolster your courage and bravery as you have evidence to support your course of action or decision making.

### CHANGE LEADERS NEED TO MAKE DECISIONS

And on that, change leaders do need to make decision. It doesn't matter whether you favour consultation or are an independent decision maker, the ability to make a decision is favoured over equivocation. The 'leader' who dithers is not well regarded in organizational life. Nor is the 'leader' who backflips. You'll be afforded one or two of these during a change without penalty, but if your leadership is characterised by an inability to make decisions or stick to them, you'll find that your followership declines.

### CHANGE LEADERSHIP REQUIRES FOLLOWERS

And on that, you need followers to be a leader.

***'He who thinks he leads, but has no followers,***

***is only taking a walk.'***

*John C Maxwell*

Your ability to lead change will be greatly enhanced by your ability to connect with the people in the organization and inspire them to follow your behaviours and your words. Think about the leaders who have inspired you – were they remote and distant? Or did they demonstrate an ability to connect with people, smile at others, ask after people? Make no mistake, this is not easy in change – you'll be very pre-occupied during this period. But you will need to prioritise connecting with people, sharing your thoughts, apprehensions and enthusiasm to build the followership.

## CHANGE LEADERSHIP CAN BE LONELY

Even with a followership, leadership can be lonely. In a pragmatic sense this is to be expected. If the organization was full of leaders, there would be the potential for anarchy and a lot of wasted energy, with people being led all over the place in different directions. There are only so many leadership roles to be filled in an organization. As a result, you can often feel lonely and isolated. My counsel is to connect with leaders in other parts of the business or permit your senior change resource to be available as a coach. You can even get an independent executive coach to help you through this time. The ability to 'offload' to a safe ear is highly valued.

## CHANGE LEADERSHIP CAN BE SHARED

Perhaps in contradiction to the point above, change leadership can be shared. What I mean by this is good change leaders look for other people in the business who have leadership aspirations and are aligned with the transformation purpose. You can deputise or call upon these people to provide change leadership in the trenches. Ideally, all your managers have some sort of formal Key Performance Indicator (KPI) around change leadership. To achieve the organization's strategy, they need to be leading their teams or departments in the direction of the changes coming through. Returning to the first paragraph in this chapter, visible and tangible support and commitment to change trumps any change communication, however sweet.

## CHANGE LEADERS NEED TO COMMUNICATE

But, on that, you do need to communicate. Your followers are looking to you to provide a high-level understanding of why are we doing this, and what will it mean. They expect you to make sense of the changes in light of the strategy of the organization. And to communicate these messages with authenticity, transparency, and clarity. Not just once, but many times. It's a very important conversation of change that you need to be initiating on a frequent basis in order to provide reassurance and confidence. If you're not saying anything, then you create a vacuum, and that vacuum gets filled with rumour and half-truths.

## CHANGE LEADERSHIP REQUIRES YOU TO EXPOSE YOURSELF

Not literally. That would be highly problematic. But figuratively. When people are feeling excited, anxious and unsure during change, they feel validated when leadership shares similar experiences. They can relate to you – and relatability creates followers and lessens the likelihood of an amygdala attack (see Chapter 12 on Neuroscience!). If you haven't already seen Brene Brown's TED talk on the Power of Vulnerability, close the book up and go and watch it. Now. Stop. Stop reading.

Okay, you're back? What did you take from it?

***'Vulnerability is the birthplace of change,***

***innovation and creativity'***

*Brene Brown*

When we get real and tap into the uncomfortable and make that public, we create a space for change to happen.

## STRENGTH BASED LEADERSHIP WORKS

Strength based leadership has emerged from the positive psychology movement. In a nutshell, it asks us to lead based on knowledge of our own strengths and by amplifying the strengths of the people around us. No person is truly excellent at everything. By understanding where your strengths lie, you can bring in people to do the aspects of your necessary work life that do not play to your strengths. When you lead teams during change by focusing on their strengths, they feel better, more engaged, and get more out of their work life. When people are in that stage, they embrace change much easier. They're not feeling threatened or criticised.

## SITUATIONAL LEADERSHIP WORKS

It's a bit old fashioned now but situational leadership theory is based on the leader's ability to adapt their style to the context of change. Hersey and Blanchard developed the theory and frameworks in the 70s. One size fits all leadership is NOT effective.

Dunphy and Stace produced a 2 x 2 model that proposes a situational leadership view of change based on scale of change and style of change management approach back in 1990. I know this dates it, but I do think it is a bit of an evergreen.

| | Fine tuning<br>Incremental adjustment | Modular transformation<br>Corporate transformation |
|---|---|---|
| Collaborative<br>Consultative | TYPE 1<br>Participative evolution | TYPE 2<br>Charismatic transformation |
| Directive<br>Coercive | TYPE 3<br>Forced evolution | TYPE 4<br>Dictatorial transformation |

TIME & VOLUME →

**Diagram 6.0: Dunphy and Stace model of contingency model of change leadership (1993)**

If you need to turn the business around in a hurry, you probably don't have time to do large scale consultation and co-creation. For most organizations, it's the time and place for a benevolent dictatorship. (post script: And I know there will be change consultants howling in dismay at that sentence and many will make the case for speedy turnarounds using their methods. I just haven't seen it. Keep an open mind and ask for client references and do your due diligence). I think there is still merit in considering this model in light of the change you want to do if only to adjust your expectations on what is required.

## ENTER ADAPTIVE LEADERSHIP

The criticisms of Hersey and Blanchards's situational leadership model and Dunphy and Stace's earlier work revolves around the assumption that you know what the solution is. With organizations moving to more agile frameworks, it's not uncommon for you to have a desire to change and need to get it started without knowing what the result will be. And in this situation, there is increased appetite for a practice known as Adaptive Leadership.

Adaptive Leadership focuses more on your ability to diagnose the situation, energise others, understand your own responses to change, and implement interventions that provide quick feedback so you can re-calibrate and course correct along the journey of change. It can be viewed as more of a facilitation process that is infused with old fashioned action research methods – change something, see how it works, do more of it, or change what you changed. The core to building resilience through this continuous change model is understanding yourself and your people so there is a much greater focus on Emotional Intelligence. You need to be able to look at things from a whole system perspective. It's worth looking at to see if there are elements of the practice that resonate for you.

## COMMAND AND CONTROL LEADERSHIP RARELY CREATES SUSTAINABLE CHANGE

Let me be clear – despite widespread antipathy to the concept now, as we are all hyper-connected and understand the limitations of hierarchy, command and control leadership is very effective at creating change. Very effective. If you're measuring your success based on, 'Did we implement a change on this date?'

Where command and control falls down during change is that it rarely generates respect for the leader, it is usually fuelled by fear, and the very nature of the top down hierarchical change means you miss many opportunities for bigger and better change. As such it's not sustainable. People revert to previous practices, attitudes and values until the next threat of consequence comes down from on high. Implementation of successful change and the realization of benefits will always benefit from consequence management. It just doesn't need command and control as the instigator of those consequences and a heavy reliance on consequence management.

## YOU DON'T HAVE TO BE BARACK OBAMA OR RICHARD BRANSON

Finally, many of the leaders I have worked with had some anxiety because they didn't fit the Barack Obama, Richard Branson mould.

The good news is you don't need to. This is simply one model of charismatic leadership and charisma is simply one tool of influence.

How else can you influence?

Being a connector – genuinely interested in the people around.

Being known for action – you get things done.

Being known for good insight – you are wise and considered.

Being known for integrity – you say what you mean, and you mean what you say.

That probably wraps up what I have observed of change leaders in my travels, let's hear from some of the others about their change leadership experiences. But remember, my change leadership mantra is pretty simple:

#justdoit.

## CONVERSATION STARTERS

**Some of the conversations you might want to have right now are:**

- Which leader has inspired you most in change – why so?
- What would it take to be more authentic in leading change? What are the risks and the payoffs?
- What would distributive leadership look like in this organization?

## IMPLICATION FOR YOUR CHOICE IN ADVENTURE

### ADVENTURE 1

- **You do not know what the change is to be,**
- **You have no internal change resources,**
- **You do have budget.**

Leading through uncertainty can be additionally fraught, but you still need to do it. Focus on what is known, and communicating the process ahead. If you remain true to your values, and your actions match with what you are saying, your audience will walk through the uncertainty with you.

### ADVENTURE 2

- **You do know what the change is to be,**
- **You have no internal changes resources,**
- **You do have budget.**

Just do it. Stay close to your change team, take their advice, and push on. Because you will need to recruit change resources in, you will have the benefit of being able to tap into stories of what effective change leadership looks like in organizations that your resources have worked in before.

### ADVENTURE 3

- **You do know what the change is to be,**
- **You have internal change resources,**
- **You do have a budget.**

Much the same as above, just do it. Talk with your internal resources about what the organization's view of leadership is and think about how that will impact your change agenda.

### ADVENTURE 4

- **You may or may not know what the change is to be,**
- **You have no internal change resources,**
- **You have no budget to hire anyone.**

Just do it. I imagine you're going to be nodding your head a bit about leadership being lonely! I would encourage you to consider carefully the concept of revealing yourself more. Through sharing your concerns and your hopes you may find you build your followership and therefore your resources.

CONVERSATION OF CHANGE WITH SIMON TERRY, CHANGE AGENT, CHANGE AGENTS WORLDWIDE:

**Dr Jen:** Simon, you have lots of experience leading change when did you first focus on the need for change management as a discipline in those initiatives?

**Simon:** Having worked in a large financial services organization for many years my early experience of change management was people approaching me with excel spreadsheets to evaluate impact and map stakeholders for their change programs. After we did that work, they tended to disappear until the change hit later. Not surprisingly I had a poor view of change management, at first.

**Dr Jen:** You are a passionate advocate now what changed your mind?

**Simon:** I was asked to lead a large customer experience transformation program as a skunk works. The CEO at the time wanted it on an accelerated timeline and wanted it to cut through the usual organizational resistance. I had a strong technology lead who convinced me that the high profile and accelerated timeline meant we needed a rigorous approach to change. We focused hard on collaborating with stakeholders to shape the vision, taking them on the journey and working through issues together. That ultimately makes change an integral and highly agile part of the execution of the program and was what enabled us to succeed.

**Dr Jen:** What is the most challenging change you have had to lead and what did it teach you about leading change?

**Simon:** I was asked to join the launch of the NAB Academy as Dean of Customer experience. My role was to report to the Australian CEO and lead a transformation of the customer experience capability enterprise wide. I had no budget, no direct reports and no formal decision making authority. I realized immediately that there were two ways to approach the challenge. I could throw my hands up and admit failure or I could see it as an adaptive leadership challenge. I took that latter path and focused on understanding the system around my role, how we could influence change and what we could get done quickly to win support and momentum in a cynical stakeholder community.

**Dr Jen:** Sounds like a challenge, what worked well?

**Simon:** Embracing the community again proved to be a strength, not a weakness. Having to win support to get anything done, made me very focused on what my stakeholder's challenges were, how they aligned to the vision and how we moved forward together. I discovered the power of holding tension. I couldn't order an outcome, but I could hold a mirror to the business to help them to see the need to change. I got very focused on building coalitions and using new collaboration platforms to get messages out and connect the organization behind the changes. At the end of the day, the influence came from delivering well and consistently.

**Dr Jen:** You work today with a number of different organizations around change and transformation initiatives what are you seeing are key issues in change leadership?

**Simon:** All organizations are looking to be more customer focused, more agile and more innovative in driving change. That's the nature of the digital economy now. Equally, businesses can no longer pretend that they aren't complex and that views of stakeholders are irrelevant. Social networks inside and outside the organization surface these issues immediately. Leaders increasingly have to manage that complexity and in ways that are less dependent on command and control and personal expertise. There is more co-creation. There is more need for transparency and autonomy. All of this pushes leaders to work more adaptively in networks and to share the load of change with their communities. At the end of the day, leadership is the ability to influence others to act. It is not about your power or your expertise. It comes down to your stakeholder's action.

**Dr Jen:** What do you recommend for anyone considering leading a change?

**Simon:** We have covered many of the points, but my key is don't try to do all the leadership work yourself. Share it around your stakeholders. Invite them to shape the change and lead that into their community. Find change agents to help you spread the word and do the work. Not only does this get the job done faster, it also produces a better outcome. Giving up control can be frightening, but it is far more effective. Working Out loud, sharing work in progress with relevant communities, is a really important way to communicate the work, find the right stakeholders and attract advocates.

**Dr Jen**: I talk about the Nike mantra of change leadership 'Just Do It", does that resonate with your experience?

**Simon:** Everyone talks about change leadership as hard. So many people have untapped leadership potential. They have a change they want to make. They are waiting for someone to authorize it. Usually their community is actually waiting for them to make the change. I encourage everyone to start small but start today. Often people are blown away to discover that most people want them to lead and to act and that change for the better is appreciated.

PART III

# Checking the Peripherals

Alrighty then, nice work. You've made your key decisions, and you've got the basics of your change initiative covered. In this section, we're going to look at some of the key topics that are taking up air time and could intrude from time to time. I don't want you to ignore them; I do want you to have as much knowledge as possible on the issues that can help you extract value, and ignore what you need to ignore with confidence. I'll also give you a chapter that summarises everything you need to know before closing the book!

# 12 Future of work practices and change management

As you progress in your adventure, you may find that your focus is interrupted by 'shiny new toys' of the organizational change kind. What I mean by that is that there's a whole stack of 'Future of Work' practices that are starting to pick up momentum in the change space. They're usually fronted by evangelists who can be very loud about why you should be including them in your workplace change considerations. The ones I am going to cover here are Agile, Neuroscience, Gamification, Work Out Loud, and Design Thinking.

I'm including these as they're my shiny new toys of preference – I've used them all, and find them very valuable. While I'm enthusiastic about them, I am not necessarily an evangelist. I remain relatively agnostic – it's horses for courses. However, you do need to know enough about the new toys to work out what to use and when.

## AGILE

By the time you're reading this book, I suspect that Agile will be the topic that's dominating most managers' conversations. You'll mention Agile and someone will snap back – do you mean capital 'A' Agile or small 'a' agile? Do you mean the Agile methodology or organizational agility? It can be a tad confusing. So, let me start at the beginning. It's really just a great big snowball.

Once upon a time, back in 2001 a bunch of software coding kind of folk were playing at a conference in Utah and lamented, if only we could just get on with our job and behave like real humans and work together, we could do everything so much faster and make real cool stuff. And they sat around created what is now known as the **Agile Manifesto** (*note the big A*). It was in essence a statement of culture that creates quality software at speed. And it was built on four values of Agile.

The four *values* of Agile snowballed to the 12 *principles* of Agile. The software companies that used this manifesto saw amazing results, which led project management folk to think if coders can do things faster and of better quality, then why can't we use this manifesto on things other than software? And so, they did.

Agile snowballed to being used in generic project methodology and was so successful that senior management said, well if coders and project teams of all kinds of types can use these principles and improve performance, why can't we use this culture for our organizations?

And the snowball just got bigger and bigger.

Essentially, operational agility (how to use an Agile methodology to do things) snowballed to a cultural agility (where we behave in an agile way). Which was kind of unique, in that usually it's the culture (or values) that precedes an operational way of being or methodology. It is perhaps a bit 'chicken and egg' in regard to which comes first, but I think this is an example of the software teams having a specific culture that was so successful it was appropriated by more than more than just software teams. What do we learn from this? Perhaps it's true that the geeks shall inherit the earth?

When it comes to Agile organizational change, many organizational change practitioners with a history of organizational development experience will tell you that 'Agile is just what we've been doing all along, there's nothing mystical about it'.

I agree with that in the sense that Agile change management is grounded in pure organizational development practice. Indeed, it takes its cues from a time before the trend of change management methodologies started to dominate, leading to artefact driven change (where your change process is determined by the artefacts you are creating, e.g. we must do a change impact analysis, we must have a change strategy document, we must have a change schedule). I do think the work Agile folk have done in marketing and packaging their practices in such short time is impressive. Organizational Development and Organizational Change management folk have had no such success.

Let's have a look at the Agile values to understand how organizational change is impacted.

### VALUE 1: INDIVIDUALS AND INTERACTIONS OVER PROCESSES AND TOOLS

This value is lived through the rituals which essential help people to interact – daily stand up meetings called 'scrums', and 'retrospectives' where you look back at a defined period of time to run through what worked, what didn't, and how to iterate with that learning.

Visual management is also an example of this value. You communicate incomplete ideas on big A3 printouts where people walk by and can observe; this creates buy-in as you encourage the discussion around A3 printout.

This practice contrasts to change management that occurs through rigid adherence to a methodology or process that seems to suggest that change management occurs in a linear fashion.

### VALUE 2: WORKING SOFTWARE OVER COMPREHENSIVE DOCUMENTATION

From a change management perspective, when we value working software over comprehensive documentation we do away with 50-page change and communication strategies and plans. It forces us to think about the Minimal Viable Product (MVP). In Agile, your quality gate is: what is the minimum viable product (or process) we can create and ship? How liberating then to think about how change and communication support in the same way; strip away the fancy stuff and the bells and whistles and critically examine what is the most effective and simple way of ensuring change occurs, or how we communicate a specific idea?

This value also is represented using collaborative communication tools to just 'do it', rather than write about it. Use Enterprise Social Networks (ESNs) like Yammer for real time FAQs rather than a perfect document that rarely gets opened. Use collaboration platforms like Trello for fully visible stakeholder issues management to everyone on the team. Ultimately, done is better than perfect. Ship it!

### VALUE 3: CUSTOMER COLLABORATION OVER CONTRACT NEGOTIATION

This value speaks to us of the power of transparency, vulnerability and trust in our change management and the power of cocreation. You may be familiar with the notion of creating a 'What's in it for me?' proposition, and the common belief that people won't change unless we show them the 'WIIFM'. This can be considered a contract negotiation. We deliver the WIIFM, you will change. But in taking this approach we can create a learned dependency that isn't sustainable. The brokering or arbitration of change is tenuous at best. The alternative is to collaborate with people involved or impacted by the change to co-create the change activity and communication. It's hard to ignore the change if you have had a role in creating it, right?

### VALUE 4: RESPONDING TO CHANGE OVER FOLLOWING A PLAN

It's been observed more than once that change practitioners and change leaders like control. To work in an agile change implementation, you need to be comfortable in relinquishing control, or recognising that control occurs through short feedback cycles that allow you to understand how well you're travelling in your sprint towards your MVP. What makes this easier for change practitioners and change leaders is data. You must use communication, engagement and planning platforms that give you real time data (readership, clicks, topics that engage, feedback) that enable you to see what is changing and how you need to respond, rather than ignore them all and follow your plan.

So much of agile change management is thinking on our feet – we are not wed to processes, frameworks and artefacts, but respectful of all. The time it takes us to write a 40-page change strategy and plan is time we could be having conversations of change with the leadership who need to champion the change. There is an old joke – 'Methodologies give people with no ideas something to do'. There is some truth in this. When I attended Agile Australia a few years back, many times I was asked 'do I follow Prosci's methodology?' and on saying no, was asked how do I knew what to do.

Agile change management is common sense – you need to be good at triaging, prioritising, being nimble, using enough of a process or framework to get momentum, and knowing when to step away and do something completely different. If you are looking at employing an agile mindset and agile methodology in your change, you will benefit by having an experienced change practitioner. To a certain extent, rigid application of processes is great for people with no expertise in change – in the absence of nothing, thank goodness for the methodology! But to know when to step away, you do need the expertise and the learning.

## NEUROSCIENCE AND ORGANIZATIONAL CHANGE

I have to say, there doesn't seem to be a LinkedIn update, bestselling list, or conference outline that isn't referencing Neuroscience and management at the moment. 'Tis très sexy! Get on board…

Rewire your recalcitrant employees' brains, make the most of that neuroplasticity and create neural pathways that support change!

Or something like that…

And while I wouldn't go as far as saying we can rewire recalcitrant employees' brains, I heartily endorse the application of neuroscience in change. A few years ago, I found myself in a full day workshop with Sue Langley of Emotional Intelligence World Wide. Sue gave us a primer on the triumvirate brain, a term which suggests the brain is segmented into three core processing areas. Note, many neuroscientists now reject this and we cover it in Chapter 13, but at a general and high level the brain does have three parts that offer three different activities. These three parts are the pre-frontal cortex which does the processing of logic and reason and the 'heavy thinking', the emotional processing centre which includes the amygdala and reacts by way of 'flight, fright and freeze' and the reptilian brain (which focuses on survival needs (sleep, sex, eating).

At the workshop, Sue walked us through David Rock's SCARF model of change. For me, it was a terrific consolidation of 18 years of formal and informal learning of communication, psychology, sociology, management, organizational behaviour and Neuro Linguistic Programming studies. Langley integrates science with well-being and emotional intelligence concepts, and it packages up really nicely. It confirmed to me why several the things I do work so well, and reminded me of opportunities to do other things a little differently.

One of the challenges to neuroscience in business is that it's just a re-packaging of what we've already known with other theories ('it's just polished up by good marketing'). I think where it moves from just good packaging is that the use of brain imaging science gives us valuable insights into what aspects of 'theory' matter in practice.

So, for instance, if you unpack the SCARF model, there is very little new in the constructs. Each of the five elements (Status, Certainty, Autonomy, Relatedness and Fairness) are critical to reducing the potential for the emotional brain to over-engage (what Daniel Goleman in his book on Emotional Intelligence refers to as the Amygdala Hijack). When the emotional brain overheats, performance suffers, as does wellbeing. As we will see below, each element has been well covered with theories dating back to the 1950's.

So, for instance…

**Status** – If you reduce threat to status, people will cope better with change. Threat to status has long been known to be a critical reason for 'resistance to change'. From a theoretical perspective, it can be explained by Mead's symbolic interactionalism, and Goffman's Presentation of Self.

**Certainty** – The brain likes certainty, and uncertainty during change is a source of great distress. Change communicators know the importance of communicating what stays the same and at the same time, communicating what changes. From a theoretical perspective, it can be explained by Festinger's cognitive dissonance theory, and Berger's Uncertainty Reduction Theory.

**Autonomy** – When people perceive they have some control over the change, they cope with it better. Uncontrolled change creates anxiety, fear, anger, and disengagement.

**Relatedness** – People trust people they can relate to. It's important to establish commonalities; people are more easily influenced by People Like Them. It's a tribal association thing hard-wired in the brain. When you are listening, and seeking to understand, you can find areas of commonality. This establishes that you are 'Like Them' and can have influence.

**Fairness** – Perceptions of fairness and justice in change processes also reduce the Amygdala Hijack. Procedural justice has received a lot of academic attention in the change management literature. For example, if you plan on downsizing you need to be clear on what the process is and the logic behind who is being downsized. The procedure of downsizing needs to be perceived as fair for it to occur effectively and for those who remain to continue to be productive.

So, the concepts and their importance in change management are not new. What is new is the packaging of the proof and the use of brain imaging machines to 'prove' what concepts matter. If you were to do nothing else as a change manager or a change leader than design your interventions based on the SCARF model, you would be in a pretty good position.

## A CONVERSATION OF CHANGE WITH LENA ROSS, OWNER, CHANGE HACKS

**Dr Jen:** Lena, how do you describe neuroscience?

**Lena:** Neuroscience would be the study of human behaviour with a scientific slant on it. With recent advances in medical brain imaging devices, we're able to delve a lot more into what the brain's thinking when certain things are happening and what emotions are taking place. Neuroscience can do more by way of actual proof. I really love this quote that says 'a neuroscientist will bring lots of human states that equals to eavesdropping on the brain' from Read Montague, and I think neuroscience is the art and science of eavesdropping on the brain and finding out what that response is.

**Dr Jen:** So, tell me, what was your entry point into neuroscience? How did you first get into it?

**Lena:** I guess I probably say I've got a learning mindset so I'm always looking out for what's out there, what the current thinking is and what the research in the field. I always had this thing in my mind that there is this paradox of change – with people who allegedly resist change and yet, if we're really hardwired to resist change, we'd still be up in the trees somewhere on the Savannah. So, I was trying to reconcile that in my mind and it was a paradox that was plaguing me for a long time. Especially because I'm so interested in anthropology and psychology and change often starts at that point of resistance.

Neuroscience explained the human response and the paradox, why people respond in certain ways and how we're hardwired to respond.

**Dr. Jen:** Can you tell us a bit about how you use neuroscience on a practical level? What does that look like in an organization away from the books?

**Lena:** Yeah, that's a really good question because one thing I always like to do, as soon as I read something is try and work out how can I make whatever it is that I've read, work – and there's two ways to look at it.

First, is how can you apply it in your personal life because we are all humans, we're all hardwired in a certain way and we also have a professional life and that personal life so it plays at I think in both spheres. If I look at how I can use it practically, the SCARF model I found was a really simple framework to apply and simple for a couple of reasons. One, it's really great mnemonic just to remember stuff.

It was an easy thing to get your head around, because SCARF says if you feel like you are compromised or you're losing one of those things you go into threat mode, but if you feel like you're gaining one of those hardwired social needs, you go into a reward response. So, it's about if your brain's not feeling good about what's happening or are you feeling threat about what's happening and I thought that's a really neat way to explain it. So, with that SCARF model in front of me, I started to think about so what can I do with change.

A simple example of this when we do a stakeholder assessment, do we even think about whether they're going into threat or reward mode? Not everyone will do the same thing. Everyone's going to have a different response and sometimes that response is resistance. Some senior stakeholders for example, with an organizational change that may result in some healthy bonuses, may get a real buzz out of the change. It's going to make them excited whereas people in other parts of the organization may not may not feel so excited about it and go into high threat. So how you know is that we can start to look at that through win and gain, or reward and loss.

That was one way and another way was in running workshops on this in a major organization. And that gained a lot of interest, because I put together this SCARF self-assessment tool and I've done a lot of them now. It's simple. I've got five lines on a page that represent the five domains (Status, Certainty, Autonomy, Relatedness and Fairness). You've got threat on one side and reward on the other. I would talk to teams about the SCARF model and their primal behaviours and responses and what that meant in regard to that change they were facing and the new information, and I would get them to plot where they were feeling in response to that particular change that we're talking about in the organization, so that we're carrying out a self-assessment. Some people were feeling very high threat in the Status space and some were feeling threat say in the Relatedness space. They felt like they were going to lose their tribe or lose the people they see every day.

**Dr Jen:** Yeah.

**Lena:** As a result of that change and then I would get them to plot it on a flipchart out the front so they could see how the whole team was feeling and we could see if there were clusters, if you like. So, one example that I did with an organizational change at a large organization, the interesting cluster that people had was around Relatedness. People didn't want to report to one of the people who did not have a strong sense of 'team'.

**Jen:** Yeah.

**Lena:** So, we were able to talk about that and by talking about that emotion, that responds to change, they're also able to label it and labelling has that fabulous way of opening up halfway to conversation and understanding without sounding overly emotional, it justifies something.

So, one of the benefits I think at an individual level was that people could understand their response to change and then they were able to see how their team were feeling. And then when I said to this particular team, 'What do you want to do with this? What do you want to do with this now?' They said, 'Well, we'd like to talk about it.'

'We'd like to talk about it moving forward with the change, we'd like to include it in our team meetings and have it as an agenda item on a regular basis so we can really unpack that emotion' And the team leader felt it was a really good way to just to get people talking.

## GAMIFICATION

Gamification has been bandied about a bit in business over the last couple of years. Basically it means using game design principles in business initiatives – e.g. customer loyalty programs, employee engagement, learning programs and, potentially, change management.

Gaming is incredibly popular because it fulfils human needs in a fun way – challenge, reward, social connection, recognition, problem solving. I found myself eating up Jane McGonigal's book 'Reality is Broken: Why Games Make Us Better and How They Can Change The World' and began to understand it more after reading the the ultimate schooling on gaming in the workplace, Luc Galoppin's epic 9 part series 'Gamers Will Save Our Economy'.

In his post 'Game based learning why does it work' – Steven Boller maps out how the elements of learning align with game principles

The four key essential elements for learning are as follows:

1. Motivation.
2. Relevant practice.
3. Specific, timely feedback
4. The ability to retrieve what we've learned when we need it.

So with that in mind, I had a crack at designing a new change readiness intervention.

I had been working on the opening of the National Australia Bank's (NAB) first Smart Store, an interesting change management challenge. The Smart Store is all digital, online and self-serve. Big on innovation, and interactive. It presents a huge shift in thinking and behavior for bankers. Their role changes to one of technology educator, as well as first point of resolution for customers. There's no hiding behind counters or screens.

So, as part of this initiative I was asked to do some work on building their capability and getting them used to the new ways of operating. Culturally, NAB Retail values customer experience, innovation and continuous improvement. It meant there was a high tolerance for 'having a go' and finding a better way of what has been done before. It meant I had to 'lift my game'. And so I did.

**#700BQuest**

**Game Goals:** players to get through an individual quest and complete tasks within a designated time frame. Player with most points and on highest level at end of the day wins.

**Objective**: Players have to gather information, absorb and apply to new context (have fun learning).

Specifically:

- Become confident with technology and digital devices
- Immerse in the potential customer experience of 700 Bourke
- Raise awareness of retail 'best practice' and transfer to their role

## RELEVANT PRACTICE

For maximum learning effect, practice needs to be contextual – mirroring the situation where the learning will be applied as closely as possible. Additionally, game design often uses avatars or specific roles as a way of making it 'safe' to try new things. When in role, you don't take it personally if you get feedback that you need to do better.

With this in mind, I contacted the customer experience team and asked them to provide me with five profiles of 'typical customers' to be expected at the new store. They came up with the goods, big time – with great details on the background, mindset and attitudes of customer personas.

I provided these customer personas to the five bankers involved and told them that on Wednesday (the day of the game), they were to come to work 'in role' – thinking, breathing, eating as that customer. At 7.30 am I sent them all an anonymous text *'This is your quest mistress – what is your role doing right now? Looking for keys? Watching people on public transport? Ordering coffee? See you in T-45 minutes'*

I suspect at that point, they worked out this was no ordinary day.

Once in at the office we gathered the team and gave them their customized iPads. Each iPad had a #700BQuest sheet loaded on them (building confidence in digital device usage). The sheet gave them the rules of the game and the order in which they had to do their quest (which was similar to a scavenger hunt crossed with a mystery shopper exercise).

### THE QUEST

Each banker had to go to a set number of retail environments (some best practice, and some not) and carry out a task which represented behaviors or skill sets they would have to do in the new store (thus addressing the element of relevant practice).

To build on the competence with digital devices, at the end of the task, the banker would have to log into their private Yammer group on the iPad and leave their reflection on what that experience was like as their customer persona and what the implications were for the new store (principle of self-expression and also the ability to retrieve what we have learnt when we need it)

As Quest Mistress I was monitoring the Yammer posts all day and provided running commentary and prompts as well as points for insight – thus providing specific, timely feedback that is continuous.

### BADGES AND LEVELS

While clear goals and objectives are intrinsically motivating, the use of points, badges and leaderboards are also key elements of game design that aid motivation.

In this game we had the senior business executives and leaders give badges to Yammer posts that showed great insight. Level upgrades were facilitated by two tasks that were extra difficult (the Joker card – go find your own retail experience) and go find a store using QR codes. The leader board was provided half way through the day.

### EPIC WIN!

It was an awesome day – the team was very competitive and it really helped with the team building (they hadn't all worked with each other). We had 37 posts in the Yammer group by the end of the day and a log of how their understanding and knowledge increased throughout the day which enabled a great 'debrief' and identification of areas that might need further attention. I was delighted – and really thrilled at the opportunity to give 'gamification' a try as part of my change management practice. If you have the time and appetite for innovation, I would recommend casting a gamification lens on your learning and change readiness activities.

## WORKING OUT LOUD (WOL)

The next shiny new toy I want to tell you about is a practice called 'Working Out Loud' or WOL.

Initiated by Bryce Williams, and championed by the brave thought leaders who explore the frontiers of the Future of Work, John Stepper and Simon Terry, 'Working Out Loud' draws attention to the practice of working publicly and collaboratively to amplify connections, networks, innovation and understanding. There's now an international #WOLweek each year. I think Simon Terry, FOW consultant and transformation agent explains the value of WOL well with the value chain of Connect > Share > Solve > Innovate.

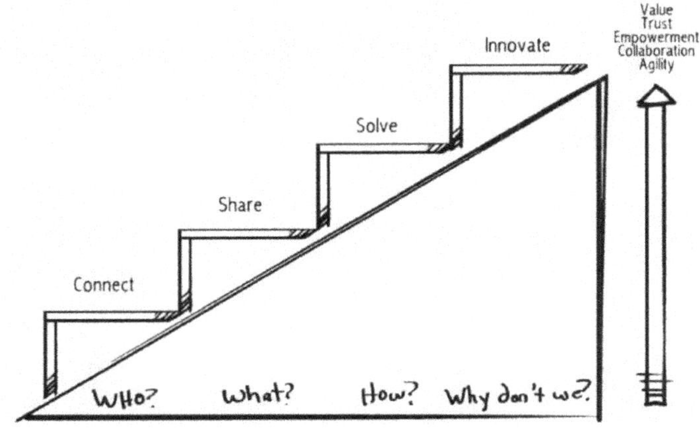


**Diagram 7.0: Simon Terry's Model of Collaborative Value**

When we 'Work Out Loud' we do so first to connect, then share, then solve problems publicly, which can lead to innovations. At its most basic, we do this by narrating our work on public platforms – posters by our desk, Yammer, twitter, or SharePoint – 'I'm working on product x– we're doing [activity]'. This increases opportunity for connection, then sharing, you get the picture.

I had heard of it a few years ago, but in thinking about getting on board with it, I was struck by how many WOL posts that felt to me like twitter did in 2008 – that self-conscious public declaration on what was being had for breakfast (or now, what I'm doing in my workday). People were trying to Work Out Loud but somehow missing the mark ever so slightly, or not sharing anything of interest – a narcissistic work diary entry, if you will. And so, I struggled with the concept. If I were to Work Out Loud, how would I ensure that the noise to signal ratio didn't get worse? Don't get me wrong, we all have to start somewhere – but I wanted to fast track! How could I make it a practice that would add value to the organization rather than just position me as another clever clogs trying something new… and how would I do it in such a way that it added value to my practice? I was working on a whole of enterprise change program in one of Australia's largest banks.

It came together when I read some of the contributions to Simon Terry's WOL in action webpage and after following conversations of fellow Change Agents within the Change Agents World Wide organization. They said:

- Take a risk
- Pick a project that people can contribute to
- Offer a genuine invitation to make it better
- Make yourself discoverable

Gold. I knew what I could do. It so happened at the same time I was working on an enterprise strategic and operational change plan to be delivered in rather complex conditions and in an accelerated fashion (*read crazy deadlines*). At the same time, I was meant to be doing tactical stakeholder engagement, issues management and reactive project communications. The change in the organization was rather high profile.

I decided to run an 'open house' on the change and communication planning. I set up for two days in a row in a meeting room from 12 pm – 4 pm and with all my work on display for comment and discussion. I shared the activity on the internal Yammer platform and positioned it honestly – *I could do with the help – big task, executing at speed, with wide reaching impacts. Come along and work with me, regardless of your experience in the change industry. If you are just curious about the project, come along and find out more.*

It was risky. There were no formal communications about the project out in the organization, so my draft messaging technically could be seen by anyone. This is not the norm for organizations where there need to be many levels of sign-off before the communications are shared. But, positioned as 'These messages are our starting point, how do the messages resonate with you?', those that visited gave great feedback. It was genuinely a project which people could contribute to.

And it was a sincere invitation. I had people come in and share their experiences of similar initiatives in other organizations, and practitioners shared other enterprise artefacts so I didn't need to re-invent the wheel. Weeks later, I was still being contacted by people who couldn't make the open house but wanted to know more or share what was going on their world (interdependencies). These were people I couldn't have known about in my initial stakeholder scans – so it gave a big tick to navigating the complex networks that we have in organizations.

There were many hours when I didn't have anyone visit, so my Working Out Loud was, well, weird... But I had all my team working in the same room, so it gave us some solid time to work through stuff together. It certainly wasn't wasted time.

I've since used the practice many times, and now in a current engagement, I've made it part of the change project methodology. Once a work package team is 60% of the way to the completion of their solution, they need to run a WOL webinar with other members of the program to share what they are doing, connect with others, ask for help in solving problems with the solution, and ultimately make it better.

I can see it being abused though – a highly scripted and controlled roadshow. I tend to think I work out loud (publicly, transparently and collaboratively) as a default practice, so it doesn't feel that risky to me. Sharing via social platforms like Yammer or Facebook does amplify the benefits, but posters on the wall and visual management are effective too. The tonality of the invitation to others to work with you matters as well. You need to genuinely *want help* from your peers. I think simply sharing what you are doing probably lacks in value; the humility and openness of exposing where people can work with you is what makes the value-add.

## CHANGE BY DESIGN

In the last five years, we've seen an increase in the popularity of 'Design' in organizations, or as it is often referred to, Design Thinking. Basically, we are asked to think about our programs as a 'designer' would. Design thinking is a human-centred, prototype driven process for innovation that can be applied to product, service, and business design (Cohen, 2014).

This resonates with me as at least half of my engagements have been a result of a poorly designed change initiative. You can save a lot of money on change implementation if you get a professional in early and design it properly.

It's even been said before that if all organizations adopted design thinking there would be no need for change management. I'm sympathetic to this view – but sceptical of how long it would be before I would be running out of work.

I'd actually argue that design thinking represents best practice change management. I think we've moved a long way from the earlier view that change management was all about implementing top down planned change. Best practice change management increasingly recognises that organisations are complex systems, and we do our best work when we create semi-structures and leave room for emergent change.

In their book 'Design thinking: understand, improve, apply. Understanding Innovation', Plattner, Meinel and Leifer propose four rules to design thinking.

- The human rule – all design activity is ultimately social in nature.
- The ambiguity rule – design thinkers must preserve ambiguity.
- The re-design rule – all design is re-design.
- The tangibility rule – making ideas tangible always facilitates communication.

All of these rules are congruent with good organizational change management. Admittedly, the desire to preserve ambiguity is not often without a fight. But this is why there is the need to create semi-structures – enough control to protect the organization from damage, and enough flexibility to allow the serendipitous discovery and emergent ideas.

Some of the key tools in design thinking are:

- Understanding your audiences' thoughts, desires, beliefs and actions.
- Co-creating outcomes with that audience.
- Creating early versions or prototypes and testing for fit / relevance / acceptability.
- Root cause analysis, five whys, mind mapping.

Again, all of these tools should be part of the change manager's tool kit and as a leader of change, you would want to see this in action. If you don't know that humans are at the centre of the changes you are introducing, you will falter. The changes will have a much better adoption rate if the audience or recipients of change have been involved in their creation. Testing is a key phase of the change processes, and we build in time to make amendments (or prototypes) if the solution is not working. We often describe a lot of our efforts as "lifting up rocks to see what's under them". This activity could also be described as root cause analysis. Good change management occurs with diligent discovery.

Now, having said this, I make no claim to be an expert in design thinking. I've worked with design thinking practitioners – I've attended a couple of conferences, read a book or two. But I do think 'design thinking' is a toy you want in your toy box!

**CONVERSATION OF CHANGE WITH HELEN PALMER, FOUNDER OF QUESTO.**

**Dr Jen:** Helen – how do you define 'design' in relation to organizational change?

**Helen:** I think some people when they hear "design" think it has to be a whole design process, with intense research, ideation and prototyping activity. Yes, that's one approach to doing design. And one I fully support in designing the change – that is the vision of something that is changed - to be implemented. Another approach is making principle-based choices as you 'design'. In my professional kitbag are useful principles, the result of other people's research and knowledge, to apply intentionally or 'by design', to make particular desirable outcomes more likely. I think this latter approach is more accessible to change practitioners, so I'll focus what I share on that.

I draw on design principles from different fields. Some from the learning design and some from the user experience and service design. I look for ways to apply them in what I'm designing. And the thing that I'm designing from a change practitioner point of view is typically the program of change, or as I like to see it, the experience of change. I see learning and change as two sides of the same coin. If people who are going through a changing experience, they're also going through a learning experience.

In organisational change you often can't predict what's going to happen, so taking a principle-based approach rather than a 'step one, step two, methodology approach', allows more freedom for addressing what's going on in the most appropriate way.

The second aspect of design is being human-centred. Doing 'human-centred design' has become a common catchphrase. It's not just design for design's sake. It's more than recognising you are serving people, its understanding that humans inherently have quirks and limits that must be considered in the design. I have a particular passion that will come out I'm sure in what I'm saying now, about a common machine-centric view of organizations. That somehow, they're an engine …

**Dr. Jen:** Finely tuned engine.

**Helen:** Indeed, and that people inside this organisational engine are a widget to plug-and-play. I think sometimes the change methodologies, or the change that's going on, have an underlying assumption that people are simply widgets in an engine. Thus change is making them to be better widgets, or taking them out and changing them for other widgets. For me, this has the sense that we will miss the beauty, the possibility of humans. Yes, with all their foibles of what might be seen as irrational, illogical behavior, but that could equally be seen as creative, spontaneous, ingenious behavior. So rather come from the point of view, "Hey, what are the realities of being human?" Start there and don't say, "Get rid of that messiness. We want rational, logical, human beings, and we're going to do training and upload what's required and get the right kind of behaviors." For me, the creativeness of an individual, and of a collective of individuals going through change, holds so much positive promise and possibility. And I want to bring that out.

**Dr. Jen:** I'm trying to imagine that conversation with a project sponsor. I'm just wondering, how does that go? Do you normally work with projects or do you work at a higher level with leaders in the organizations?

**Helen:** It's more at the project level. I want to have more of these conversations at the strategic level because I think that's where you can get in early enough to set the right kind of tone and approach on a project. If you come in later, then there's an expectation, that managing change will be a bit of training and communications. I think, wrong! Wrong approach. Wrong level. Wrong. Wrong in so many ways. It's about, having a human view upfront of how we are going to view people.

To your question about how do I introduce it, I don't go in saying, 'I'm going to do design'. I think that sets off all kinds of unhelpful reactions. What I will say is, 'I'm going to think about what's going on in this organization, and inquire and engage with people before I give you any kind of strategy or documents. If you're expecting me to come in in week one and produce a document to put in your hands, then I'm not right for your organisation.' There will probably be a time in the process where it makes sense for me to put a strategy together. The designerly approach is to be guided by what is fit for purpose and for the specific organisational context.

I remember one sponsor in a university project saying, 'So what I want is email sent out on a fortnightly basis'. And I thought, 'Okay. What I know about universities are, everybody gets emails, so many emails, with so many words in them. Emails are often completely ignored or overlooked'. So I ask, 'Let me understand: You'd like some smart communications that cut through all the organisational noise? Well, email is unlikely to achieve that in your organisational context.' Sometimes when I can share an example like that, their reaction gives me a sense of their appetite for thinking differently about things. That's partly what design is. It's not, we're going to do things following each step of this methodology. It's asking, what kind of situation do you have here and what's fit for this purpose? Let's find the elements to best address that. Resourcefulness can play a really useful part here too. It could be that you have an amazing group of people here, if we could find and empower them, we could have a bunch of really effective change champions. And that would be a better way to invest our time and our engagement, rather than focusing on how many messages to send and what channels to use. Writing good messages and using digital channels are definitely useful things to have in your toolbox, but design is about having the conversation at a higher order thinking about what you are trying to achieve. Why are we sending an email? It's to communicate. Why are we communicating? It's to engage. What's the engagement about? We want to win the hearts and the minds of people.

Let's just think, how many hearts and minds have been won by the recipient of an email in your inbox telling you what's going on?

It's about putting the proposed action in the context: Who are these people? What kind of cultural landscape are we working in? What's the appetite for messages and engagement? If you've a situation where people are against the coming change, constantly communicating by email, a method with significant emotional distance, is not going to positively change their sense of their workscape. Such a situation needs more relational type activity. Whereas if you have a situation with a light, uncontroversial change, then maybe email's appropriate. It's 'horses for courses'! I won't know what I would be best to advise until I've talked to people around the organisation, and discovered out what resources are available. Then one sense of the design aspect comes in - I expand my vision to find and utilize what already exists and use it for best effect.

**Dr. Jen:** You mentioned before learning design principles, can you give me an example of how that might play out on a recent engagement in terms of what were the learning design principles that you used?

**Helen:** There's various levels of learning design principles, but one that can be very useful is Cognitive Overload – that people who are cognitively overloaded cannot absorb new input. When I'm designing a learning event, I make choices like: Shall I talk for 60 minutes on a particular piece of content? Or should I talk for 10 minutes and then have an activity to engage and play with idea I've talked about? The latter is better for minimising cognitive overload. Choices about how to engage without overloading can be a consideration for a short period of time in the classroom, to across a whole program of change. If the outcome you want from a particular communication is that people are sufficiently informed to act in a desirable way, then consider what might be useful ways to inform people without cognitively overloading them. You may have decided to send an email, but now you need to consider how much goes in the email. It's unfortunately common that senders of email will cram everything they want to share in a single email which becomes a short novel! A better email might be a succinct invitation to come to an information session where people can ask the questions that they particularly want answered, rather than be pushed a lot of information that we want to give and they might not want or need. Well-designed communication is not just about what people want to know, it's also addressing factors like: How much can they take in right now with all the other organisational noise around? Which time is the best time for them to pay attention to what they are asked to attend to? Would they do better to read, listen or watch to fit their personal capacity to absorb new information? That's an example of rethinking engagement with the principle of Cognitive Overload in play.

**Dr. Jen:** I see. You also mentioned user experience and UX is not typically a space that plays into the change management field, although some could argue that it should or maybe it does with different language, I don't know. Tell us about user experience and design.

**Helen:** Experience is an interesting word because most people when they say 'UX' think of a piece of technology and the experience of engaging with that technology. Sometimes it's seen as it's a little more than interface design. Interface design might be the graphical elements on the screen, and experience design is seen as, what was your experience in using that? Is it, on one level useable and intuitive and at another level, delightful and pleasurable? I take some of that thinking and ask, what if experience design was about the interface between a person and the change that's going on in the organization. Let's reuse those principles and envisage the entire program of change as an experience, rather than a series of communications that are disseminated. With an experience lens, we might consider, that first part of the experience is acknowledging that something has been lost or will be left behind. You might consider what's a natural experience that you've had where there's been loss and grief, maybe a funeral? I'm not saying you turn your change program into a funeral, but you might consider the human experience of a situation like that, for the things we do as humans in rituals and symbolism, that help us move through a stage of loss.

In another circumstance, where something new is launched, you might create a celebratory experience analogous to a party with invitations, great catering, nice music, festive decorations, and a sense of joy and pride. Take the elements from a common human experience, and overlay or incorporate them into a part of the change program. Simply doing a bunch of comms and training to serve functional purpose can feel sterile and bereft of a sense of, well, humanness! As a real living breathing human, want to be enthralled. Or to be challenged. Or to be consoled.

**Dr. Jen:** That really taps into the human centric side of it there.

**Helen:** Absolutely. There's recognizing, hey as humans we want to be enthralled, and in grief we want to be consoled. I think sometimes in organizations, there's a parental stance of 'You will do this because I told you so'. Or a dictatorship, 'I'm in charge here and I say this will be the change and you all just fall into line, if you want a job, fall into line'. I think, organisations don't have to take a stance like that. As the leader of the organization, I may not recognize but I could get in the headspace of recognizing, I have a high levels of agency and influence with the change that's going. So what might it be like for people in my organisation who have less of an agency or influence? I believe it's important to get an empathic understanding of other people's actual or likely experience of the change ... here we are back in design territory. Design methods include ways to get a deeper understanding of where people are at and what kind of readiness there is to change.

Taking a human-centred design approach requires consideration of human factors. One category of human factors is the Physical. When people are stressed, stuff is happening to them at a physical level - physiologically, adrenaline is being dumped into their system to help them cope. That's just the reality of being human. And there's lots evidence from science that tells us it's very hard to pay attention and take on new information when you've got adrenaline pumping into your system. To consider the Physical human factor in change, there are practical things to encourage people to do to avoid or overcome stress: like Go for a walk; Breathe fresh air; or take extra vitamin B. Caring actions such as these can be built into the change experience because you recognize that external change impacts on the internal experience a person has. A well-designed change experience could do things that mitigate or minimize negative feelings and experiences, and amplify or extend positive ones. It's an oldie and a good advice: Accentuate the positive, eliminate the negative!

## CONVERSATION STARTERS

**Some of the conversations you might want to have right now are:**

- Which of these shiny new toys might we want to consider?
- What else are we hearing about that we need to do some research on to determine fit for our change project?
- Do we have any 'in-house' resources who have expertise in FOW practices?
- If we chose to ignore FOW practices, what are the costs associated with it?

## IMPLICATIONS FOR YOUR CHOICE IN ADVENTURE

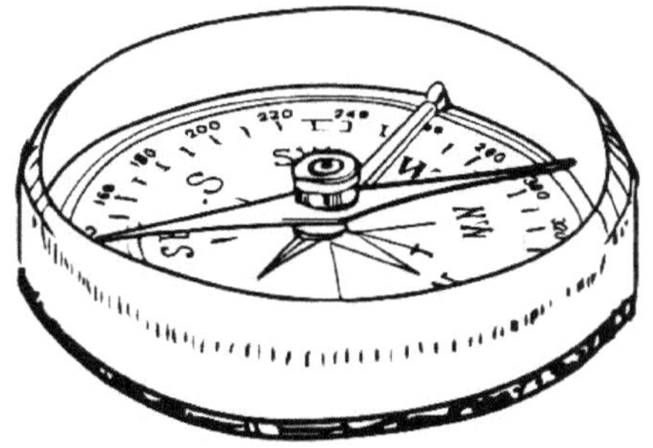

## ADVENTURE 1

- **You do not know what the change is to be,**
- **You have no internal change resources,**
- **You do have budget.**

Future of Work practices provide you with some great tools in handling uncertainty. Work Out Loud allows you to open to a broader group and help gain clarity. Design Thinking and Agile methodologies both lend themselves to empathy for the end-user / impacted audience and hypothesis driven testing. This means you can firm up clarity with low risk.

### ADVENTURE 2

- **You do know what the change is to be,**
- **You have no internal change resources,**
- **You do have budget.**

It may be that the resources you recruit have their own shiny new toys. When they introduce the shiny new toy to you, ask for examples of where it works well and where it doesn't. You want someone considered in their use of FOW practices.

### ADVENTURE 3

- **You do know what the change is to be,**
- **You have internal change resources,**
- **You do have budget.**

The use of FOW practices in your change work may not be widespread or you may find your internal resources have invested in next practice learning and have an expanded tool box. Use the conversations starters to find out what everyone's experience is in FOW, and whether it might be worthwhile in investing something new.

## ADVENTURE 4

- **You may or may not know what the change is to be,**
- **You have no internal change resources,**
- **You have no budget to hire anyone.**

Working out Loud will be your friend! If ever there was a time to work transparently and publicly within your organization to gain assistance and co-creation it is now!

Now, with your head full of the possibilities of 'next practice' it's time to move to the debates and myths that may distract you on your journey. The next chapter takes you through six of the topics that often are hotly contested, and how you could benefit from the context in your change implementation.

# 13 The myths and big debates of organizational change

Chapter 13 is about the myths and big debates in organizational change. There're quite a few of them and they often distract from the task at hand. People get very heated in defending their position on these, and the people who are feeling defensive may be on your change team. Here's what you need to know about six of the big debates, other than the '70% of change fails' myth.

If you have read Chapter 5, you will be aware that I have had a role in debunking the '70% of change projects fail' myth. This was a few years ago now, and you know what? I'm getting increasingly uncomfortable with the practice of myth busting. Primarily, I'm concerned we are throwing babies out with the bathwater.

Here's what I am thinking.

Too many times I'm seeing people refer to the myth with 'Well, that's just a myth and doesn't mean anything anymore …' with a casual indifference to the creative destruction cycle (e.g., once something is destroyed, something must be created in its place). Imagine how unhelpful it would be if you went to your change leader on your own initiative and said 'Hey, I've just read that 70% of change projects fail', and your change leader responds with 'No, that's just a myth, it's not true.' *And walks away.* Here's the thing – at that point in time, your concern is real. It needs to be addressed as such.

I ended my myth busting post with a call to action, and a subsequent post on how we should define success (in Chapter 5). Yet I'm not hearing the myth busting conversations evolve along this line. The myth busting is just a metaphorical slap down. End of conversation.

The other thing that has me uncomfortable is the belief that if science can't (hasn't) proved it, it can't be true. I just don't buy that – I think there are many things in life that will never be proven scientifically but just feel right or true to us. There are many things that we don't yet know how to study scientifically. AND I know I used a scientific research argument in my 70% post...

And this is where I think we need to move the conversations of myths to: what is the utility of this myth? Why has it taken purchase? If it is so ingrained in our organizational life, what could (should) we retain and use?

In that vein, let's look at some of the others.

### THE KUBLER ROSS / SATIR INSPIRED LIFECYCLE OF CHANGE

This is a popular model used in change. It's a combination of Kubler Ross's work on the emotions people experience when faced with those who have loved ones who are dying (so experiencing loss) and Virginia Satir's model of five stages of change.

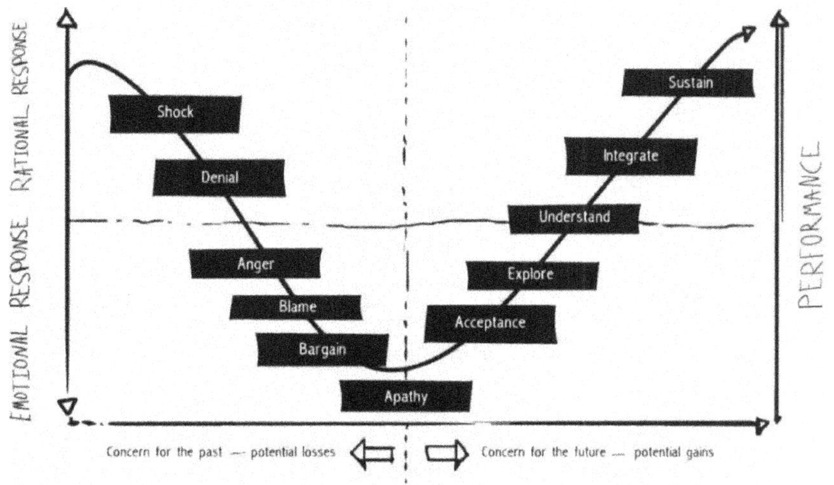


**Diagram 8.0: Lifecycle of change**

When used in change management, it presents a picture of how people can move through a process of emotionally adjusting to loss, and come to a point of experimentation and adoption of the change. When faced with change that incurs loss, everyone moves through the curve – some go deeper than others, and some move more slowly than others. What's important in this image is the productivity baseline. While people are experiencing emotions related to change that keep them down, that change is making your people less productive.

Those in the 'anti' camp will tell you it was never empirically proven as a model of death and dying. They will tell you it paints an overly negative and pessimistic model of change. That it does not account for learning cycles, resilience, well designed change, and assumes that everyone goes through this cycle. Practitioners who use it with clients are frowned upon and whispered about in snarky tones (much like I use with those who use the 70% myth…)

But you know what – I use it frequently. One, because I believe that it is a very valid representation of what I see happening in many organizations. Believing that it's true doesn't prevent me from including appreciative inquiry approaches or designing for learning cycles and innovation. And two, because it has utility.

It helps me:

- explain what change management does (change management makes the curve skinnier and shallower)
- explain why I need leaders to step up and lead and resource change (you risk under performance while people move through the curve)
- set expectations and make sense of things (don't be alarmed if you see this. This is great, you can see this group has moved through the curve to the point of experimenting)
- involve your people in co-creation – they are less likely to design a change with unacceptable loss.

It may not be proven by science, but my *anec-data* (*which would be data comprised of anecdotes and stories*) would suggest there is a lot to heed from it. And yes, I'm aware that I will have a cognitive bias that means that I'm selecting anecdata that supports the model.

## TRAINING PROGRAMS NEED TO BASED ON THE 70:20:10 BEST PRACTICE MODEL OF LEARNING

The 70:20:10 best practice model of learning is based on the concept that people do most of their learning through experience (70%), some of their learning through a boss or more senior peer (20%), and a little bit through formal education (courses). It makes sense and conveniently justifies that our organizations don't need to fund formal training and development for employees – just make sure the work they do is challenging enough! It also suits workplaces where it is very difficult to pull people off shop floors or customer spaces to do formal training.

But a 2014 article '70:20:10 Where is the evidence?' by Andrew Jefferson and Roy Pollock in the Association of Talent Development Science in Learning Blog reveals that like the 70% of Change Fails Myth, the 70:20:10 model has sketchy origins and no empirical evidence to back it up.

Okay, what do you do with this then? Clearly it resonates with many – and you will need to be thinking about how you do training as part of your change program if there are new processes, behaviours or software to learn. My advice is to stick with a tried and true learning needs analysis. Have a considered discussion with your Learning and Development people to work through what needs to occur with regards to development and what is the optimum mix to produce that outcome. It will vary from organization to organization based on culture, the type of work that is done, and the budget available. At worst, this model gives you three options to consider in your planning.

## NEUROSCIENCE IS BEING MISUSED IN CHANGE

As I covered in Chapter 12, neuroscience is having a considerable impact on change management. Basically, the advent of medical imaging machinery (for example MRIs) to measure the brain's activity has resulted in a lot of assertions about what is true and what is not, and fairly faddish application of this to management practice. Neuroscientists are getting increasingly nervous about the 'clumsy' use of the studies to justify management consultants' advice. Many of the statements that consultants are using in neuroleadership, change management, and neuromarketing are not proven in empirical research – although they do make for great press!

I get that scientists are uneasy about its use in business. We're being told things like 'We can re-wire people's brains so they like change'. And that's a bit of an overstatement. I do find considerable benefit from using a few the principles from neuroscience studies in change work as we covered in the previous chapter. Again, I accept they may not be proven scientifically. However, models like David Rock's SCARF resonate. Claims of re-wiring recalcitrant employees' brains take it a bit too far.

Here's my understanding (and remember, *not a neuroscientist*). Our brains crave certainty. This means change is often uncomfortable for us. Our brains are also 'plastic' – that is, capable of creating new neural pathways. But we need to be willing to do this work AND this often takes many years. Creating new neural pathways for employees in the period of time you would want to is unlikely – not without targeted brain-washing. That's generally not in the change manager's or change leader's tool kit.

So, I think how I would summarise this is, studies of neuroscience and human behaviour can be insightful for how we manage change. Dogmatic adherence and hopes of a magic bullet are probably not going to get you too far. Keen an open mind brain.

## PEOPLE INHERENTLY DISLIKE CHANGE

This one is a partial myth. Partial in so much as we covered above that our brains privilege certainty over change, and change can result in anxiety for people. Particularly an unexpected change that triggers a strong emotional response.

But here's the thing – it really depends on two things: What the change is, and how the change is executed. Telling someone they've won a million dollars and won't have to work again will result in massive change. I'm willing to bet that person is pretty comfortable with it. Telling someone that you are clawing back their flexible work from home policy is not likely to have the same impact. Context matters.

Equally, an eagerly anticipated change (new computers, new furniture, a better process to submit reimbursements) that is poorly executed will also be frustrating. As we covered in Part 2, poor communication, inadequate consideration of capability and little leadership will reinforce that people don't like change. Conversely, giving people the opportunity early in the change to be involved and have some ownership of what is to come, and even unattractive change can be handled well.

## YOU NEED TO CREATE A BURNING PLATFORM TO ACHIEVE CHANGE

This is SO not true. It's actually an interesting distortion of a fairly famous change metaphor first raised by change management guru Daryl Conner in his book *Managing at the Speed of Change*. As the story goes, in 1988 Conner was watching a TV news program on the Piper Alpha oil rig platform disaster which included an interview with Andy Mochan, a superintendent on the oil rig. In the interview, Andy recounted how he knew that to stay on the rig was to definitely perish, and to jump into the fiery seas was to face probable death. It was an unenviable choice and one that required significant commitment and determination to face. Conner reflected on this, and it occurred to him it was a terrific metaphor that leaders often face – to do nothing is to perish, to do something is also risky and they often don't wish to do it. It takes extraordinary commitment, yet results in successful change.

Over time, this metaphor was spread globally and there are now many variations of it. It most often gets trotted out to say that we need to create a burning platform so that people will jump. Not quite. In fact, a little fool hardy to manifest anything so traumatic. You do need to ensure there is a strong reason why change is required and the leaders do need to be committed even if there is risk. But no creating fires, okay? Life is interesting enough without it. Daryl Conner writes about how the metaphor was misappropriated in his post 'The Real Story of The Burning Platform' and how there are different ways of using the original one.

## YOU CAN'T USE CHANGE CHAMPIONS ANY MORE

So, one of the dominant issues in the change field is that change champions have been over- used and are no longer effective. This one is worth heeding in my view, but let's again not throw babies out with bathwater! It will be important for you to find people who are natural champions of the change you want to create who will advocate on your behalf. Where it gets tricky is the deliberate identification of people who *should* be a change champion.

Inevitably the same people get tapped on the shoulder, and it's always because they're influential, great communicators, and their roles span many organizational boundaries – they can get around and evangelise. But here's the thing. If the same people are continually being tapped on the shoulder to be change champions, their impact wears a little thin AND they start to fall behind on their day job and lose their enthusiasm for change advocacy. We need to be really careful about this practice.

The alternative is to activate the social architecture. This is a relatively new concept popularized by Belgium Change Management expert Luc Galoppin. It draws upon community building principles. Luc describes the social architecture as:

'There is more to organization than what is just in an organization chart and that there is something specific about the white space in between the boxes and the lines of the organizational chart. And something that happens there that makes an organization think. When I zoom in on that part of an organization and I discover that that's composed of different layers and those layers are a different type of communities and dynamics already present there in that organization that I can work with. I don't have to work against them, I can work with them and that work, my research into that so to speak is called social architecture'

And what that to me is finding the 'tribes' that are naturally aligned to your change and introducing the change to them first. You do away with reliance on core people and provide a compelling invitation to a community to become engaged in your change.

## CONVERSATION STARTERS

**Some of the conversations you might want to have right now are:**

- What does *anec-data* tell you about the change myths in your organization?
- If you dug deep into those myths what might be driving them?
- What might be a reason for their stickiness?
- How do the myths and debates mentioned in this chapter impact your current initiative?

## IMPLICATIONS FOR YOUR CHOICE IN ADVENTURE

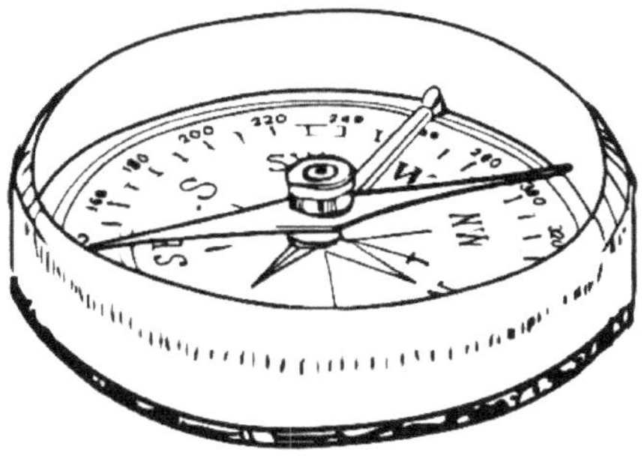

### ADVENTURE 1

- **You do not know what the change is to be,**
- **You have no internal change resources,**
- **You do have budget.**

Until you've solidified what the change will be and locked in your budget it wouldn't be wise to spend too much time engaging in discussions of these myths and debates. These will potentially be something to look at once you're well underway and you have some resources. It would be good to explore in context of your own organization – perhaps there's a myth that 'You can't change something if you don't know what it is'?

### ADVENTURE 2

- **You do know what the change is to be,**
- **You have no internal change resources,**
- **You do have budget.**

Given you understand the change to implemented, it may be worth doing an initial scan of these debates and myths with respect to, how do they play out in your initiative? Does your initiative result in loss? Is there a way to minimise that to ensure productivity (co-design?)? What are the implications for training and development? Is there a way to use some of the insights of neuroscience without being slavishly dependent on what has been published?

## ADVENTURE 3

- **You do know what the change is to be,**
- **You have internal change resources,**
- **You do have budget.**

I think this would make for a great change-team brown-baglunch. Convene your resources and put the myths and debates on the table to debate. Which resonate and why? Which bear more utility? What other change myths exist within your own organization that you could unpack? In having this conversation you'll be building the teams' capability – exposing them to information they may not have known and building their confidence in critical thinking.

## ADVENTURE 4

- **You may or may not know what the change is to be,**
- **You have no internal change resources,**
- **You have no budget to hire anyone.**

Okay, so if anyone comes near you with talk of myths and 'that's not true', tell them to put up or shut up! Unless they're prepared to offer you some of their time in resourcing, they don't get to throw smack downs. To be honest, you have enough of a challenge on your plate. I would not be paying much attention to any of the myths and debates. Part two needs to be your focus.

Now with your head full of the possibilities of 'shiny new toys' and myths and debates, it's time to consider your next steps. The next chapter takes you through what might be next for you in terms of your change management experience.

# 14 Where to next?

***'Education is the most dangerous tool***

***for those that wish to change the world'***

*Nelson Mandela*

Well kudos to you. You've braved it almost all the way to then end. And you still want to be accountable for driving change in your organization. You're my kind of change agent!

I'm conscious that some of you at this point may wish to go further. Perhaps this experience will ignite a career change for you, because you've recognise a calling. Or in managing the change resources in your initiative, you'll be asked to sponsor them in further professional development.

So, in responding to that interest and desire, this chapter finishes up by looking at what are your options for further professional development and engagement in the change management arena.

## ACCREDITATION

Increasingly, we've seen a demand from clients and organizations for 'accredited' change management practitioners. This is understandable. Accreditation provides reassurance, and a calibration of skill level. You know if you secure a CPA this person will have a minimum level of skills in the accounting field.

Accreditation also looks great on a resume. It's a shortcut in the hiring process.

However, accreditation does not replace experience and wisdom. I remain uncomfortable with the false assurance that they may give an organization about a person who has one. Accreditations are part of a larger portfolio of values in conjunction with personal attributes, experience, and disciplinary study (either formal or informal). If your company will pay the big dollars for it, then terrific, grab the opportunity.

Currently, if you want a change management accreditation here are some of the following options (there will undoubtedly be more based on your region):

| Who | How many days | Pre-requisite experience | Cost | Format |
|---|---|---|---|---|
| ACMP – Certified Change Management Professional (CCMP) | Not a training based certification | Yes | $595 – $745 USD for application | Essays & Multiple Choice Exam reviewed by Assessors and aligned to the ACMP Standard |
| APMG Foundation | 3 days | No | $1695 (AUD) | Exam |
| APMG Practitioner | 2 days | Foundation | $1395 (AUD) | Exam |
| CMI Foundation | N/A | No<br><br>Does need to be mapped to CMI competences | $1250 (AUD) | Written submission and proof of education |

| | | | | |
|---|---|---|---|---|
| CMI Master Part 1 | | 5 years' experience | $1095 (AUD) | Written submission and proof of experience / education |
| CMI Master Part 2 | | 5 years' experience | $1495 (AUD) | Practical examination |
| PROSCI Certification | 3 days | No | $5950 (AUD) | Presentation on day two and a multiplechoice exam on day three |
| PCI | 3 days | No | $3500 (AUD) | Team based presentation on case study |

**Table 3.0: Accreditations and certifications**

### POST GRAD EDUCATION

Most people will get access to organizational change theory in management degrees where there is a major in organizational development, or a business degree that has a major in organizational change. There are not that many dedicated degrees in organizational change management. This may change in the future if there is sufficient demand on those that set the curriculum.

So, your options become:

- Do you wish to enrol in a single subject or a selection of subjects just for the education (may not be allowed by many Universities)?
- Do you wish to undertake a Master's degree and select change subjects being offered or seek out a dedicated Graduate Diploma?

- A couple of things to think about or ask here:
- What are the criteria for enrolment – will my cohort have work experience from which to draw upon in class discussion?
- What format is the subject / degree run in (e.g., intensive, online, distance, or do I need to commit to a weekly presence during semester)?
- Has the lecturer worked in change management before, or is the knowledge base theoretical?
- And then what are your needs – a fundamental theoretical base, or cutting edge, what's on the horizon?
- Are there guest lecturers or current cases being used in the teaching?
- How does the teaching staff ensure relevance?

By way of explanation of this last point: the cycle of academic publishing means that by the time you are reading an article in a quality journal, the research will have been conducted many, many years earlier. In some cases, 10 to 15 years. It may be more useful to have a reading list that includes white papers, industry reports, blogs, and conference papers to keep a mix of contemporary knowledge of change management as well as the classics.

Can you speak to alumni or past cohorts? How have they used what they learnt?

## PROFESSIONAL DEVELOPMENT CONFERENCE & COURSES

Another option is to invest in your own professional development via conferences, masterclasses and courses. If your organization is not paying for these, in some countries you will find these a tax deduction for professional development.

These courses will cost anywhere between $400 – $6000, and run from half a day to five days. Many of the professional accreditation vendors will run versions of these. Again, caveat emptor – look very carefully at the credentials of the provider, and ask for contacts of previous cohort / participants. Most of these will be interactive; if you wish to sit passively in a course and download information, then you may be disappointed.

### PROFESSIONAL ASSOCIATIONS

As we discussed in Chapter 2, there are two major professional associations that are covering organizational change management (ACMP, CMI), and while both have made big inroads in developing formalized 'bodies of knowledge', their memberships are modest relative to the number of people working in the space. Becoming a member of these can be useful if you want to find more people to network with and have curated content shared with you. There will usually be discounted tickets to networking events, conferences and professional development.

### COMMUNITIES OF PRACTICE

You will also find that within your city there may be a semi organized community of practice. LinkedIn will be useful for finding this out, as will platforms like meetup.com. In 2009, I co-founded a local community of practice for those working in change management roles, The Change Management

Professionals (not to be confused with the Association of Change Management Professionals, we just chose the name first!). This community of practice continues to meet on a quarterly basis.

There are also organized networks such as the CMI, OD Network, and Appreciative Inquiry Network to consider. Existing Professional Associations in management, governance, and HR maybe considering special interest groups too. Ask them. Dedicated change management recruiters also host community events, so look them up as well.

## SOCIAL MEDIA

Don't disregard social media either; there is an emerging community on Twitter in the field, and multiple groups on LinkedIn. You may find some of the contributions quite limited, but you'll also find contributors who really build your knowledge.

Here's a list of tweeters and bloggers you may wish to follow / favourite.

## CHANGE TWEEPS

@jasonlittle – tweeting since 2008, author, blogger, podcaster, involved with Spark the Change conferences, agile OCM

@jenfrahm – yes, me. You should be following me. Tweeting since 2008, author, blogger, podcaster, Communications and OCM, smattering of Future of Work and agile OCM, #CAWW

@enclaria – tweeting since 2009, author, blogger, consultant and podcaster, TEDxer, primarily OCM

@carolinekealey– tweeting since 2009, blogger, developer of the Results Map, OCM and Communication

@simongterry – tweeting since 2009, blogger, co-founder of International Work Out Loud Week, Charter Member of Change Agents World Wide (#CAWW), change with a heavy dose of Future of Work and ESN

@gailseverini– tweeting since 2009, blogger, owner of the Organizational Change Practitioners group, primarily OCM and thought leader in Strategy Execution, exemplary connector

@lucgaloppin tweeting since 2009, founder of Organizational Change Practitioners group, driver of #socialarchitecture in change

@changefactory – tweeting since 2009, blogger, primarily OCM

@changemblog – tweeting since 2013, blogger, editor of Change Blog, primarily OCM

@lenaemelyross – only tweeting since 2015, but definitely one to follow – OCM + future trends

@helenbevan – tweeting since 2010, Chief Transformation Officer with the NHS, #CAWW

**BLOGGERS**

- Bryan Gorman, http://changementor.net
- Change Agents World Wide http://blog.changeagentsworldwide.com/

- Faith Forster, Pinipa, http://www.pinipa.com/blog/
- Gail Severini, The Change Whisperer, http://gailseverini.com/
- Heather Stagl, http://www.enclaria.com/resources/blog/
- Jason Little, Agile Coach, http://agilecoach.ca
- Joe Gergen, Once more unto the change, http://intothechange.net
- Lena Ross, http://www.lenaross.com.au/#!blogs/vikss
- Luc Galoppin, Reply-MC, http://www.reply-mc.com/
- Martin Fenwick, http://www.thechangefactor.com/our-blog/
- Matthew Newman, People Change, http://change-man/peoplechange
- Torben Rick, http://www.torbenrick.eu/blog/
- Gilbert Kruidenier, Kruidenier Consulting, https://www.kruidenierconsulting.com.au/blog
- Anthony DoMoe, Anthony DoMoe, http://www.anthonydomoe.com/
- Wendy Hirsch, Wendy Hirsch, http://wendyhirsch.com/blog-1/
- Doh. Me. I thought it was a given. Apparently not! The Watercooler @ http://conversationsofchange.com.au

## EXTERNAL COACHES

If you don't have a mentoring option within your organization, either formal or informal, you may wish to make a case for external coaching. This is where you engage someone who is external to your organization on a regular basis to assist you in developing your change capability and knowledge. Again, like the first two options, the would-be coach should be able to provide contact details of previous coaching clients who can tell you what they got out of it. You'll need to be clear on whether you are looking for a formal executive development program internally, or more of a reflective listening and wise counsel service.

### SELF-STUDY

There is such a rich resource out there in libraries and bookshelves. If you are serious about developing your knowledge, read widely and regularly. Start with the classics like the following list:

- How to Win Friends and Influence People – Dale Carnegie (1936)
- The Change Masters – Rosabeth Moss Kanter (1983)
- 7 Habits of Highly Effective People – Stephen Covey (1989)
- The Fifth Discipline – Peter Senge (1990)
- Managing at the Speed of Change – Daryl Conner (1993)
- ADKAR: A Model for Change in Business, Government and Community: How To Implement Successful Change in Personal and Professional Lives – Jeff Hiatt (2006)
- Managing Organisational Change: A Multiple Perspectives Approach – Ian Palmer, Richard Dunphy, and Gib Akin (2009)
- Managing Transitions: Making the Most of Change – William Bridges and Susan Bridges (2009)

- Switch: How to Change when Change Is Hard – Chip Heath and Dan Heath (2010
- Leading Change – John P Kotter (2012)
- The Heart of Change: Real Life Stories on How People Change Their Organizations – John P Kotter and Dan S Cohen (2012)

**LinkedIn Groups**

Join a few LinkedIn groups and spend some time digesting their discussions. You can start with CMI, The Change Source, Organizational Change Practitioners, Allegra, Change Management Professionals. There are of course others. Reach out to your peers and ask them which groups they find valuable.

## CONVERSATION STARTERS

**Some of the conversations you might want to have right now are:**

- Should I as the initiator / leader of this change upskill further? Or am I comfortable with the team I have assembled.
- Given building change capability internally assist implementation should I be sponsoring more activities to develop change management internally.
- What are my team's views on further professional development in the field?

## IMPLICATIONS FOR YOUR CHOICE IN ADVENTURE

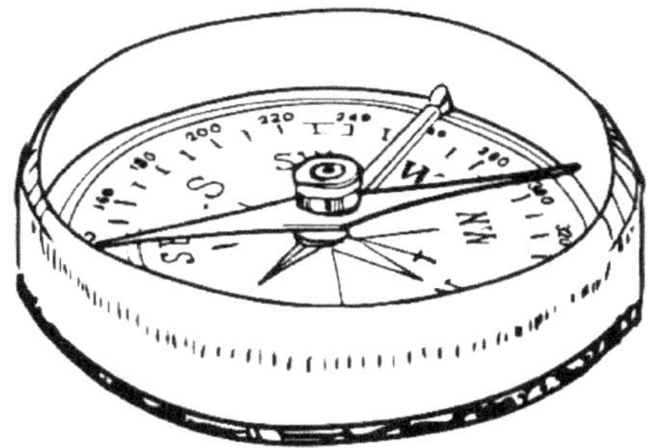

### ADVENTURE 1

- **You do not know what the change is to be,**
- **You have no internal change resources,**
- **You do have budget.**

This chapter will be useful to you if, as you are progressing, you decide you want to further develop your career in change management, especially the self-study options. You may not want to be a fully accredited change manager but the books and communities may be beneficial.

### ADVENTURE 2

- **You do know what the change is to be,**
- **You have no internal change resources,**
- **You do have budget.**

Like Adventure one, this chapter could be useful to you if you find you really enjoy the experience and want to go further. Re-read this chapter before recruiting if you can – it will help you make sense of the resources that come your way.

### ADVENTURE 3

- **You do know what the change is to be,**
- **You have internal change resources,**
- **You do have budget.**

Given you have internal resources, this might be best used to understand where they can go for further development. If you find that you have been enthralled by the experience you might want to change career?

### ADVENTURE 4

- **You may or may not know what the change is to be,**
- **You have no internal change resources,**
- **You have no budget to hire anyone.**

This chapter provides you with some communities and online resources which could provide extremely useful from a self-serve perspective. You're just going to have to carve out time for it.

# 15 The adventures you have chosen

We've been through a lot of stuff so far, and your head is probably full to bursting with so much information if you have read from start to finish. But you know what, I know there's a few of you who have just skipped straight to the end. Cheeky. To think I slaved all those many nights on words for you.

For the benefit of both types of readers, here's a summary of what I think are the important points for each the Adventurers. There will be some overlap as some things are common to each of you, but other points would be more relevant to an Adventurer travelling a certain path.

## SUMMARY OF ADVENTURE 1: UNCLEAR WHAT THE CHANGE IS, NO RESOURCES AND HAS BUDGET

Not knowing what the change is the first difficulty you face. Someone in senior management has most likely said something like 'Things have got to change' without being specific about what that change should be.

Chapter 2 addresses the jargon and big areas of conflict in organizational change that may trip you up as you start off. As you will most likely to be engaging a change consultant to help you shape up what you want to do and how you will do it, this chapter should empower you to ask your change consultant some defining questions about their approach. It will also assist you in evaluating their proposals and statements of work as to their fit for purpose with your engagement.

Chapter 3 covers the main roles in change work. As you start to change up what the change is likely to be with your change consultant, this will be a handy guide to thinking through who will do what. It will help you to temper considerations of what you are defining is feasible given your resourcing profile.

Chapter 4 looks at the implications of recruiting change resources and establishing the Return on Investment (ROI) of your change initiative. This should provide you with a guide on what to look for in a consultant and some clues on how to engage. Talk with your peers outside of your company to understand who they have used and how effective they were.

Chapter 5 is your call to set yourself up for success. In this instance, purpose becomes your true North. As you navigate your way through the initial conversations of change, shaping up the design of the solution to your problem, you will benefit from regularly checking the alignment to purpose. If you are unclear what the change is, it is important consider milestone-based success measures. It will be difficult to establish an installation or benefits realization metric upfront. This will become clearer as you progress though. Initially, you will want to focus on the process of change as your area to measure. In working through the uncertainty and ambiguity, how are your people feeling? What is the level of contribution you are seeing? What is the implications of all this talk about change on their productivity?

Chapter 6 covers methodologies and frameworks. Given where you are you may want to work with a more emergent change methodology. Appreciative Inquiry will be a good one for you as will Lean Change, as the feedback cycles can help you shape what the ultimate change vision is.

Chapter 7 calls upon you to consider change capability. Without it you will be pushing uphill. An assessment of your organizational change capability will be very important in designing what your change will be and how you introduce it. You may end up moderating your ambition if the change maturity assessment reveals that you're not ready for the change.

Chapter 8 raises the questions of change readiness – will they, and can they? Like organizational change capability, a presumptive assessment of your organizational change readiness will be helpful in the design of your change. Ultimately though, change capability is more important than change readiness. Without change capability, you are unlikely to shift the dial on change readiness.

Chapter 9 talks to change resistance and stakeholder engagement. Ah, the excitement of a clean slate to work with. Okay, so forget about change resistance completely, and in designing what your change will be, make sure you have done a very thorough stakeholder identification activity and stakeholder engagement plan. This will set out who your stakeholders are, what their concerns are with the change and how you will address them.

Chapter 10 addresses change communication. Initially, a formal monologic change communication program isn't as important as defining your change, and ultimately it will be through dialogic change communication that you can achieve this purpose. Make sure you look at the options for co-creation – including people in conversation about what the issues are and the potential approaches. Through this strategy, you can start to test key messages and identify your audiences.

Chapter 11 covers off Change Leadership. Leading through uncertainty can be additionally fraught, but you still need to do it. Focus on what is known, and communicating the process ahead. If you remain true to your values, and your actions match with what you are saying, your audience will walk through the uncertainty with you.

Chapter 12 is the start of the last section. It is a big chapter that takes you through four Future of Work (FOW) practices and the implications for your change work. Future of Work practices provide you with some great tools in handling uncertainty. Work Out Loud allows you to open to a broader group and help gain clarity. Design Thinking and Agile methodologies both lend themselves to empathy for the end-user / impacted audience and hypothesis driven testing. This means you can firm up clarity with low risk.

Chapter 13 challenges you to consider some of the myths and big debates in implementing change. Until you've solidified what the change will be and locked in your budget it wouldn't be wise to spend too much time engaging in discussions of these myths and debates. These will potentially be something to look at once you're well underway and you have some resources. It would be good to explore in context of your own organization – perhaps there's a myth that 'You can't change something if you don't know what it is'?

Chapter 14 finishes up with considerations on what's next for you if you have really found this exciting! This chapter will be useful to you if as you are progressing you decide you want to further develop your career in change management, especially the selfstudy options. You may not want to be a fully accredited change manager but the books and communities may be beneficial.

*

## SUMMARY OF ADVENTURE 2: CLARITY ON CHANGE TO BE IMPLEMENTED, NO RESOURCES, AND BUDGET

Chapter 2 addresses the jargon and big areas of conflict in organizational change that may trip you up as you start off. In this instance, your immediate need is to recruit. Understanding what the common misunderstandings are will help you navigate engaging with a recruiting agencies or directly with candidates.

Chapter 3 defines the roles in change management. As you recruit your new team, you know now that you need to recruit not just change managers, but change communicators and change agents. You will also want to give some consideration to change sponsorship and leadership. If this is not you, you will need someone in this role. Together with your new team you can work through the remainder of the roles and ensure you have them allocated. Reread Chapter 3 again to understand the optimum composition of the resources you need to recruit.

Chapter 4 looks at the implications of recruiting change resources and establishing the Return on Investment (ROI) of your change initiative. This should make life a little easier in recruiting your new team. I would be heading to a specialist recruiting firm on this one for someone in your position – you have enough on your plate to deal with.

Chapter 5 is your call to set up for success. You're starting with clarity on the change to be implemented, which can be very useful. But have you leapt ahead without considering purpose? If the change makes no sense to your people from a heart and soul level, success is going to be challenged. As you recruit and on-board your change resources, the definition of success needs to be an overt and open conversation with them as, ultimately, how you define the success of your initiative becomes their performance metrics (e.g., are they effective in achieving these results). Be very clear that the metric you are using for change is aligned with the duration of time you have them around – if you have not included them in the design of the change, it is less likely you can measure their performance with the success of your change. Similarly, if they are contractors or internal resources who are not around to do the embedding work, it is unfair to align their performance metrics with your benefit realization.

Chapter 6 addresses methodologies and frameworks. If you're recruiting resources, then you probably want to understand what methodologies influence them. If they can't talk to any methodology – or are not able to map out for you their (semi) structured approach to change – proceed with caution. In saying this, I don't want to imply that all change should be structured, far from it. There needs to be room for emergent change and synchronicity! However, someone who is not cognizant of the general stages of their logic may prove challenging from a success standpoint.

Change 7 calls upon you to consider change capability. Without it you will be pushing uphill. You're most likely bringing in external change resources. You want to have explicit conversations about transfer of knowledge and capability, otherwise you might see a success spike which occurs during the change implementation period when the resource is there, but declines when they leave the organization.

Chapter 8 raises the questions of change readiness – will they, and can they? One of the things to discuss with your change resources is when and how to assess change readiness. As you do have budget, you may be able to resource the assessment and interventions post assessment. Probably, one of the most important considerations in this discussion is the level of survey or assessment fatigue or availability of platforms to poll people.

Chapter 9 speaks to change resistance and the importance of stakeholder engagement

If you have brought change resources in from outside, they will most likely want to start with a stakeholder identification process and be asking a lot of questions about the stakeholders' position on the change. This means that you are already addressing change resistance – either current or potential. You're in good hands. Keep the focus on frequent engagement and looking at how to ensure the organization is ready for change.

Chapter 10 addresses change communication. This chapter will be helpful for you to review with your change communication resource. You don't need to develop a change communication plan or strategy, that's their job. But they do need to have considered the concepts and observations covered in this chapter.

Chapter 11 covers off Change Leadership. Just do it. Stay close to your change team, take their advice, and push on. Because you will need to recruit change resources in, you will have the benefit of being able to tap into stories of what effective change leadership looks like in organizations that your resources have worked in before.

Chapter 12 is the start of the last section. It is a big chapter that takes you through four Future of Work (FOW) practices and the implications for your change work. It may be that the resources you recruit have their own shiny new toys. When they introduce the shiny new toy to you, ask for examples of where it works well and where it doesn't. You want someone considered in their use of FOW practices.

Chapter 13 challenges you to consider some of the myths and big debates in implementing change. Given you understand the change to be implemented, it may be worth doing an initial scan of these debates and myths with respect to: How do they play out in your initiative? Does your initiative result in loss? Is there a way to minimise that to ensure productivity (co-design?)? What are the implications for training and development? Is there a way to use some of the insights of neuroscience without being slavishly dependent on what has been published?

Chapter 14 finishes up with considerations on what's next for you if you have really found this exciting! Like Adventure one, this chapter could be useful to you if you find you really enjoy the experience and want to go further. Re-read this chapter before recruiting if you can – it will help you make sense of the resources that come your way.

*

## SUMMARY OF ADVENTURE 3: CLARITY ON CHANGE TO BE IMPLEMENTED, INTERNAL RESOURCES, YOU HAVE BUDGET

Chapter 2 addresses the jargon and big areas of conflict in organizational change that may trip you up as you start off. This chapter is great for you – you can really cut to the chase with your internal resources to understand how they operate and make sense of their world. The conversation starters at the end of the chapter will be particularly useful in framing up your initial conversations with them. The time you invest in this mutual sense-making will pay big dividends!

Chapter 3 covers the roles in change management work.
Sometimes when you have internal resources, there are things that are just taken for granted. Using this list in this chapter will help you work through the various roles and ensure that you and your change resources are on the same page.

Chapter 4 looks at the implications of recruiting change resources and establishing the Return on Investment (ROI) of your change initiative. This chapter provides a list for you to evaluate your internal resources so you understand their strengths and skills sets. If they don't have the requisite experience and skills, you may need to make a case for external recruiting. Share this chapter with the Resourcing Manager to help facilitate a conversation on who you might be able to have on your team.

Chapter 5 is your call to set up for success. You, too, need to do a quick check on alignment with purpose. You are all set up to go, but it will be a false start if the change is not aligned with the broader purpose of the organization. Check with your internal resources on how they have measured success in the past. It may be that measuring success is unfamiliar to them and it will be useful to go through the ROI exercise to formulate messaging for your stakeholders on why this is initiative is so important (e.g., the costs of not doing it). Do lead a conversation with them on what they have seen work well in the organization before – what is the optimum recipe for success?

Chapter 6 covers methodologies and frameworks. In this instance, you may already have a preferred methodology within your organization, either bespoke or commercial. It's probably worth having a chat with your resources about how they have used the methodology successfully in the past, and ask them about where they think there are limitations. This will be a very insightful discussion.

Chapter 7 calls upon you to consider change capability. Those on Adventure 3 have a higher-level change maturity and change capability than other adventurers by virtue of the fact that there is already a recognised need for change management in the creation of change resources. It will be important to work with your change resources to understand what the change radar looks like – what else is landing at the same time as you wish to so that you're not overloading the business with change. This may not be a problem if you have a very high change maturity though; this might be a very agile organization.

Chapter 8 raises the questions of change readiness – will they, and can they? Have a chat with your internal resources about what they have done in the past to assess change readiness, and do they have formal milestones in a change process where they review change readiness. If they don't and haven't, perhaps show them this chapter and ask to them to come back to you with their recommendations.

Chapter 9 speaks to change resistance and the power of stakeholder engagement

Okay, the tricky bit with internal resources is sometimes they are so used to their internal stakeholders they have blinkers on about what the sources of change resistance are. Conversely, they often have a deep understanding of the business concerns. Your job here will be to make it safe enough for them to tell you about the 'elephant' in the room, the real reason why people may be uncomfortable with the change, and to push them to take a fresh look at their stakeholders.

Chapter 10 addresses change communication. Again, this chapter will be useful to talk to your internal resources with. Encourage them to a 'change communication lessons learned' and identify the pitfalls they've seen in your organization. Ask them 'What is the change communication campaign you would have wanted to implement, but weren't allowed to?' Their answers may surprise you.

Chapter 11 covers off Change Leadership much the same as the other adventures – 'just do it'. Talk with your internal resources about what the organization's view of leadership is and think about how that will impact your change agenda.

Chapter 12 is the start of the last section. It is a big chapter that takes you through four Future of Work (FOW) practices and the implications for your change work. The use of FOW practices in your change work may not be widespread or you may find your internal resources have invested in next practice learning and have an expanded tool box. Use the conversations starters to find out what everyone's experience is in FOW, and whether it might be worthwhile in investing something new.

Chapter 13 challenges you to consider some of the myths and big debates in implementing change. I think this would make for a great change-team brown-bag-lunch. Convene your resources and put the myths and debates on the table to debate. Which resonate and why? Which bear more utility? What other change myths exist within your own organization that you could unpack? In having this conversation you'll be building the teams capability – exposing them to information they may not have known and building their confidence in critical thinking.

Chapter 14 finishes up with considerations on what's next for you if you have really found this exciting! Given you have internal resources, this might be best used to understand where they can go for further development. If you find that you have been enthralled by the experience you might want to change career?

*

**SUMMARY OF ADVENTURE 4: YOU MAY OR MAY NOT KNOW THE CHANGE TO BE INTRODUCE, YOU HAVE NO RESOURCES AND NO BUDGET**

Chapter 2 addresses the jargon and big areas of conflict in organizational change that may trip you up as you start off. This chapter provides you some guidance in understanding what phases of change are that you need to plan for with the blunt and crass outline of what methodologies do. Role clarity is probably a bit easier for you – for now, you are it. You are accountable and there is probably not much ambiguity about that – although you are encouraged to be thinking about who you could co-opt from your peers to form a working party that fills these roles! To that extent, it doesn't really matter how you define organizational change management. I am hoping that though that you have got some good insights into the things you want to be thinking about with your change.

Chapter 3 delves into role clarity in change further. While I have said, 'for now you are it', this chapter may be helpful to you in realizing that you don't have to do it all alone. In understanding the different roles, you may be able to put names to the role and start some influential conversations of seconding people into new positions with you. Ever the optimist.

Chapter 4 looks at the implications of recruiting change resources and establishing the Return on Investment (ROI) of your change initiative. It may be that the section on calculating ROI may be the most valuable part of this book to you – and will enable you to revisit the need for a budget and then how to recruit. Failing that, use the attribute list to think about who exists in the organization at the moment who meets those attributes – you may have an ally lurking around.

Chapter 5 is your call to set up for success. So, I'm guessing someone has a pretty strong agenda for change to put you in this position. Change must happen. Start with that person and have a conversation on what the purpose of the organization is and how does that align with the need to change, and the ability to not resource the change. If that conversation fails to change your circumstances then you need to look at the enablers of success with an eye for frugal ingredients.

You can still measure success – it may be that your success is just more modest than others. Reality checks will be very important.

Chapter 6 provides an overview of common methodologies and frameworks. If your conversation on ROI has not been successful, I'm going to say in this situation, get yourself accredited in a commercial methodology quick smart. You're going to have a lot to think about and at least you will have a recipe to follow.

Chapter 7 asks you to consider change capability. I think we can safely assume that you are in an organization with relatively low change maturity and change capability. It doesn't have to stay this way; it may be that with the content in this chapter you can be at the vanguard of innovation and change in your organization.

Don't be overwhelmed by it – you are building from scratch so now is the time to consider these foundation elements.

Chapter 8 raises the questions of change readiness – will they, and can they? With no budget, and no resources, you're in a bit of a bind, but I think it's important you do at least one review of change readiness before you make the decision to go-live. You will most likely need to rely on qualitative feedback – ask your business unit leaders to lead a discussion on the topic and report back to you. If you have an Enterprise Social Network (ESN) like Yammer, maybe you could initiate a public discussion – as are we ready for this change?

Chapter 9 talks to change resistance and the power of stakeholder engagement. This will be an interesting space for you to work in as good stakeholder engagement is time intensive and you will most likely be tempted to just focus on rolling out this change. All I can offer you now is assurance that the more time you put into stakeholder engagement, listening to concerns, responding to these concerns, the better you will be when it comes to launching this change.

Chapter 10 addresses change communication. I'm hoping this chapter is useful to you in thinking through what the purpose of your change communication is and the varying ways you can approach it. You may struggle with execution, so I would encourage you to soak up the next chapter on Leadership and simply communicate with as much transparency and frequency as you can.

Chapter 11 covers off Change Leadership. Just do it. I imagine you're going to be nodding your head a bit about what was said about leadership being lonely! I would encourage you to consider carefully the concept of revealing yourself more. Through sharing your concerns and your hopes you may find you build your followership and therefore your resources, and people who will help you on this quest.

Chapter 12 is the start of the last section. It is a big chapter that takes you through four Future of Work (FOW) practices and the implications for your change work. Working out Loud will be your friend! If ever there was a time to work transparently and publicly within your organization in order to gain assistance and co-creation it is now!

Chapter 13 challenges you to consider some of the myths and big debates in implementing change. Okay, so if anyone comes near you with talk of myths and 'that's not true', tell them to put up or shut up! Unless they're prepared to offer you some of their time in resourcing, they don't get to throw smack downs. To be honest, you have enough of a challenge on your plate. I would not be paying much attention to any of the myths and debates. Part two needs to be your focus.

Chapter 14 finishes up with considerations on what's next for you if you have really found this exciting! However, at this point this chapter provides you with some communities and online resources which could provide extremely useful from a self-serve perspective. You're just going to have to carve out time for it.

# Conclusion

And there you have it, my friend. You've reached the end of the book.

Thank you for investing time in this quest – I hope that you are feeling more confident in your ability to introduce change into your workplace, select the right resources, and evaluate quality in change delivery.

People have been on at me for years to write a book on change management. I couldn't see how I could add value to the considerable volume of publications on change until I realised that the piece that was missing was the practical 'Jiminy Cricket' on the shoulder of the manager / leader who didn't know how to start. Not unlike the many requests I get for change management coaching. As such, this book represents a consolidation of the queries I've received and the help I've been asked for.

If you have a question that has not been resolved in this book,

I welcome it at the Conversations of Change Facebook page, or email me. You just might see the answer emerge in a future blog post or podcast.

Yes, for those who simply haven't got enough and want to get more there are five options:

1. Like the Facebook page
2. Follow me on twitter
3. Sign up for the Change Nugget series
4. Subscribe to the podcast series
5. Connect with me on LinkedIn

Just head over to **www.conversationsofchange.com.au** to connect.

I genuinely believe that change doesn't have to be as uncomfortable as many organizations seem to experience. I would love this book to land in the hands of more managers who are about to implement change – imagine a world where people in organizations just get on with change!

## HELP ME ON THIS QUEST

If through reading this book you have found that you will save money by making a better selection of your change resources, save time because you have a better sense of what to focus on, and/or save anxiety and stress because you feel more confident or empowered, I would love to you share your impressions on LinkedIn, Twitter, Facebook, your internal enterprise social network (Slack, Yammer, Chatter) or write a review on Amazon.

But for now, thank you. Good luck with your change! Let me know how you go.

**#jointhechange**

# Reference list

Reference list.

Armenakis, Achilles A., Stanley G. Harris, and Kevin W. Mossholder. 1993. 'Creating Readiness for Organizational Change.' *Human Relations* 46 (6): 681–703. doi:10.1177/001872679304600601.

Ashkenas, Ron. 2013. 'Change Management Needs to Change.' *Harvard Business Review*. April 16. https://hbr.org/2013/04/change-management-needs-to-cha.

Barney, J. 1991. 'Firm Resources and Sustained Competitive Advantage.' *Journal of Management* 17 (1): 99–120. doi:10.1177/014920639101700108.

Beck, Kent, Mike Beedle, Arie van Bennekum, Alistair Cockburn, Ward Cunningham, Martin Fowler, James Grenning, et al. 2001 'Manifesto for Agile Software Development.' *Agile Manifesto*. http://agilemanifesto.org/.

Bhargava, Rohit. 2011. 'The 5 Models of Content Curation.' *IMG*. March 31. http://www.rohitbhargava.com/2011/03/ the-5-models-of-content-curation.html.

Blanchard, Kenneth H, Patricia Zigarmi, and Drea Zigarmi. 2000. *Leadership & the One Minute Manager: Increase Effectiveness by Being a Good Leader*.

Bokeno, R. M., and V. W. Gantt. 2000. 'Dialogic Mentoring: Core Relationships for Organizational Learning.' *Management Communication Quarterly* 14 (2): 237–70. doi:10.1177/0893318900142002.

Bottom Line Performance. 2012. 'Game Based Learning: Why Does It Work.' *Lessons on Learning*. October 20. http://www.bottomlineperformance.com/game-basedlearning/#_edn3.

Bovey, Wayne H., and Andy Hede. 2001. 'Resistance to Organizational Change: The Role of Cognitive and Affective Processes.' *Leadership & Organization Development Journal* 22 (8): 372–82. doi:10.1108/01437730110410099.

Brown, Brené. 2010. *The Power of Vulnerability*. TED.com. https://www.ted.com/talks/brene_brown_on_vulnerability.

Change First. 2012. 'The ROI for Change Management.' https://www.changefirst.com/roi-change-management/.

Change Management Institute. 2012. 'Organisational Change Maturity Model.' *Change Management Institute*. February. https://www.change-management-institute.com/organisationalchange-maturity-model-2012.

Change Management Review. 2016. '5 Next Generation Thought Leaders.' https://twitter.com/chgmgmtreview/status/751049780218851328.

Cheney, George, Lars T Christensen, Theodore E Zorn, and Shiv Ganesh. 2004. *Organizational Communication in an Age of Globalization: Issues, Reflections, Practices*. Prospect Heights, Ill: Waveland Press.

Cohen, Rueven. 2014. 'Design Thinking: A Unified Framework For Innovation.' *Forbes*. March 31. https://www.forbes.com/sites/reuvencohen/2014/03/31/design-thinking-a-unified-frameworkfor-innovation/#636f1add8c11.

Conner, Daryl. 2012. 'The Real Story of the Burning Platform.' *Connor Partners*. August 15. http://www.connerpartners.com/frameworks-and-processes/the-real-story-of-the-burningplatform.

Cooperrider, David L, Peter F Sorensen, Therese F Yaeger, and Diana Whitney. 2001. *Appreciative Inquiry: An Emerging Direction for Organization Development*. Champaign, Ill.: Stipes.

Dunphy, Dexter, and Doug Stace. 1993. 'The Strategic Management of Corporate Change.' *Human Relations* 46 (8): 905–20. doi:10.1177/001872679304600801.

Fallon, Nicole. 2014. '30 Inspiring Leadership Quotes.' *News.com.au*, November 22, sec. Business News Daily. http://www.news.com.au/finance/work/leaders/30-

inspiringleadership-quotes/news-story/da92d9dc5a26b00544924ca3950b78a4.

Frahm, Jennifer. 2005. 'The Impact of Change Communication on Change Receptivity: Two Cases of Continuous Change.' Queensland University of Technology. http://eprints.qut.edu.au/16124/1/Jennifer_Frahm_Thesis.pdf.

———. 2017. 'The Water Cooler.' http://conversationsofchange.com.au/water-cooler/.

Galoppin, Luc. 2010. 'Gamers Will Save Our Economy.' *Reply MC*. August 2. http://www.reply-mc.com/2010/08/02/gamerswill-save-our-economy/.

———. 2011. 'Social Architecture (a Manifesto).' *Management Innovation Exchange*. July 13. http://www.managementexchange.com/hack/social-architecturemanifesto.

Gergen, Joe. 2014. 'The Adventures of a Secret Change Agent.' *Once More Unto the Change*. February 13. https://intothechange.net/2014/02/13/the-adventures-of-a-secretchange-agent/..

Goleman, Daniel. 2006. *Working with Emotional Intelligence*. Bantam trade paperback reissue ed. New York: Bantam Books.

Gryger, Liz, Tom Saar, and Patti Schaar. 2010. 'Building Organizational Capabilities: McKinsey Global Survey Results.' *McKinsey&Company*. March.

http://www.mckinsey.com/businessfunctions/organization/our-insights/building-organizationalcapabilities-mckinsey-global-survey-results.

Hammer, Michael, and James Champy. 1993. *Reengineering the Corporation: A Manifesto for Business Revolution.* 1st ed. New York, NY: HarperBusiness.

*How to Deal with Resistance to Change Heather Stagl TEDxGeorgiaStateU.* 2015. YouTube. TEDx Talks. Georgia State University: TED.com. https://www.youtube.com/watch?v=79LI2fkNZ2k.

Hughes, Mark. 2011. 'Do 70 Per Cent of All Organizational Change Initiatives Really Fail?' *Journal of Change Management* 11 (4): 451–64. doi:10.1080/14697017.2011.630506.

Jefferson, Andrew, and Roy Pollock. 2014. '70:20:10: Where Is the Evidence?' *Association for Talent Development.* July 8. https://www.td.org/Publications/Blogs/Science-of-LearningBlog/2014/07/70-20-10-Where-Is-the-Evidence.

Kealey, Caroline. 2015. 'Best Practices in Change Communications.' Results Map. http://www.resultsmap.com/wpcontent/uploads/2015/05/Best-Practices-in-ChangeCommunications-2015.pdf.

Kotter, John P., and Leonard A Schlesinger. 2008. 'Choosing Strategies for Change.' *Harvard Business Review.* August. https://hbr.org/2008/07/choosing-strategies-for-change.

Kotter, J.P. 1996. 'Leading Change.' Harvard Business School Press. http://www.hbs.edu/faculty/Pages/item.aspx?num=137.

——. 2008. 'A Sense of Urgency.' Harvard Business School Press. http://www.hbs.edu/faculty/Pages/item.aspx?num=34979..6

Kübler-Ross, Elisabeth, and Ira Byock. 2014. *On Death & Dying: What the Dying Have to Teach Doctors, Nurses, Clergy & Their Own Families.*

Lewin, Kurt. 1947. 'Frontiers in Group Dynamics: Concept, Method and Reality in Social Science; Social Equilibria and Social Change.' *Human Relations* 1 (1): 5–41. doi:10.1177/001872674700100103.

Little, Jason. 2014. *Lean Change Management: Innovative Practices for Managing Organizational Change.* Happy Melly Express. https://www.amazon.com.au/Lean-Change-ManagementInnovative-organizational-ebook/dp/B00O580KUI.

Machiavelli, Niccolò, and N. H. Thompson. 1992. *The Prince.* Unabridged. Dover Thrift Editions. New York: Dover Publications.

Makar, A. B., K. E. McMartin, M. Palese, and T. R. Tephly. 1975. 'Formate Assay in Body Fluids: Application in Methanol Poisoning.' *Biochemical Medicine* 13 (2): 117–26.

McGonigal, Jane. 2011. *Reality Is Broken: Why Games Make Us Better and How They Can Change the World.* New York: Penguin Press.

Nohria, Nitin, and Michael Beer. 2000. 'Cracking the Code of Change.' *Harvard Business Review*. June. https://hbr.org/2000/05/cracking-the-code-of-change.

Piderit, Sandy Kristin. 2000. 'Rethinking Resistance and Recognizing Ambivalence: A Multidimensional View of Attitudes toward an Organizational Change.' *The Academy of Management Review* 25 (4): 783. doi:10.2307/259206.

Plattner, Hasso, Christoph Meinel, and Larry Leifer, eds. 2013. *Design Thinking: Understand – Improve – Apply*. Understanding Innovation. Heidelberg: Springer.

PROSCI. 2006. 'Prosci's ROI of Change Management Model.' September 11. http://www.change-management.com/ProsciROI-of-Change-Management-Tutorial-110906.pdf.

Rock, David. 2009. 'Managing with the Brain in Mind.'*Strategy+Business*. August 27. https://www.strategy-business.com/ article/09306?gko=5df7f.

Rogers, Everett M. 1962. *Diffusion of Innovations*. New York: Free Press.

Ross, Lena, and Grant Ross. 2012. 'Change Hurts: Myth or Reality?' Change Hacks. http://media.wix.com/ugd/d48dfa_48d8131252794a6eacb752c7aacbe502.pdf.

Sandberg, Sheryl. 2013. *Lean in: Women, Work, and the Will to Lead*. First edition. New York: Alfred A. Knopf.

Sanders, T. H., H. E. Pattee, and J. A. Singleton. 1975. 'Lipoxygenase Isozymes of Peanut.' *Lipids* 10 (11): 681–85.

Satir, Virginia, ed. 1991. *The Satir Model: Family Therapy and beyond*. Palo Alto, Calif: Science and Behavior Books.

Schworm, Peter. 2013. 'Nelson Mandela's 1990 Visit Left Lasting Impression.' *The Boston Globe*, December 7, sec. Metro. http://www.bostonglobe.com/metro/2013/12/07/mandela-visitboston-high-school-left-lasting-impression/2xZ1QqkVMTbHKXiFEJynTO/story.html.

Severini, Gail. 2012. 'Change Management Methodology (Strategy Execution Methodologies Series. Post 4).' *Change Whisperer*. August 16. https://gailseverini.com/2012/08/16/change-management-methodology-strategy-execution-seriespost-4/.

———. 2013. 'Optimizing Internal and External Change Management (Presentation and Tip Sheet).' *Change Whisperer*. April 19. https://gailseverini.com/2013/04/19/optimizinginternal-and-external-change-management-presentation-andtip-sheet/.

Stagl, Heather. 2017. 'Influence Change at Work Toolkit.' *Enclaria*. http://www.enclaria.com/toolkit/.

Stepper, John. 2015. *Working out Loud: For a Better Career and Life*. New York: Ikigai Press.

Waddell, Dianne, and Amrik S. Sohal. 1998. 'Resistance: A Constructive Tool for Change Management.' *Management Decision* 36 (8): 543–48. doi:10.1108/00251749810232628.

Weick, K. 1993. 'The Collapse of Sensemaking in Organisations: The Mann Gulch Disaster.' *Administrative Science Quarterly* 38.

——. 1999. 'Conclusion: Theory Construction as Disciplined Reflexivity: Trade-Offs in the 1990s.' *The Academy of Management Review* 24 (4): 797–806.

Wernerfelt, Birger. 1984. 'A Resource-Based View of the Firm.' *Strategic Management Journal* 5 (2): 171–80. doi:10.1002/smj.4250050207.

Woodman, R W, and W A Pasmore. 1987. 'Appreciative Inquiry in Organizational Life.' In *Research in Organizational Change and Development*, 1:129–69. Stamford, CT: JAI Press.

**Reading List.**

Bridges, William. 1991. *Managing Transitions: Making the Most of Change*. Reading, Mass: Addison-Wesley.

——. 2004. *Transitions: Making Sense of Life's Changes*. 2nd ed. Cambridge, MA: Da Capo Press.

Carnegie, Dale. 2007. *How to Win Friends & Influence People*. New York: Pocket Books.

Conner, Daryl. 1993. *Managing at the Speed of Change: How Resilient Managers Succeed and Prosper Where Others Fail*. 1st ed.

New York: Villard Books.

Covey, Stephen R. 2004. *The 7 Habits of Highly Effective People: [Powerful Lessons in Personal Change]*. 15 anniversary ed. London: Simon & Schuster.

Frahm, Dr. Jennifer. 2017. *The Transfomation Treasure Trove — Series I & II*. Conversations of Change. http://conversationsofchange.com.au/the-transformationtreasure-trove/.

Hammer, Michael, and James Champy. 1993. *Reengineering the Corporation: A Manifesto for Business Revolution*. 1st ed. New York, NY: HarperBusiness.

Heath, Chip, and Dan Heath. 2010. *Switch: How to Change Things When Change Is Hard*. 1st ed. New York: Broadway Books.

Hiatt, Jeff. 2006. *ADKAR: A Model for Change in Business, Government, and Our Community*. 1st ed. Loveland, Colorado: Prosci Learning Center Publications.

Johnson, Spencer. 1998. *Who Moved My Cheese?: An Amazing Way to Deal with Change in Your Work and in Your Life*. New York: Putnam.

Kanter, Rosabeth Moss. 1983. *The Change Masters: Innovations for Productivity in the American Corporation*. New York: Simon and Schuster.

Kotter, John P. 1996. *Leading Change*. Boston, Mass: Harvard Business School Press.

———. 2014. *Accelerate: Building Strategic Agility for a Faster Moving World*. Boston, Massachusetts: Harvard Business Review Press.

Kotter, John P., and Dan S. Cohen. 2012. *The Heart of Change: Real-Life Stories of How People Change Their Organizations*. Boston, Mass: Harvard Business Review Press.

Palmer, Ian, Richard Dunford, and Gib Akin. 2009. *Managing Organizational Change: A Multiple Perspectives Approach*. 2nd ed. Boston: McGraw-Hill Irwin.

Sandberg, Sheryl. 2013. *Lean in: Women, Work, and the Will to Lead*. First edition. New York: Alfred A. Knopf.

Senge, Peter M. 2006. *The Fifth Discipline: The Art and Practice of the Learning Organization*. Rev. and updated. New York: Doubleday/Currency.

# About the author

Dr Jen Frahm (PhD Management) has worked across multiple industries and professions:

- from wine sales to wedding dresses,
- veterinary products to energy retailers,
- nuns and engineers
- big banks, small IT companies.
- publicly listed, privately owned and non-profit organizations.

Her change projects have included culture change, process change, digital transformation, legislative change, mergers and acquisitions and technology / systems change and covered more than 250,000 employees.

Previously an academic, Jen's research interests cover organizational theory, organizational change, organizational communication, and qualitative research methods. She has lectured and taught over 10,000 students.

Jen's community work with the International Association of Business Communicators (IABC) Victoria Chapter, the Organizational Change Management Practitioners Group, and the Change Management Professionals has placed her at the forefront of world developments in change management and communication.

She has been listed in the Change Management Review's 5 Next Generation Thought Leaders, and Change Source's the Top 20 Change Visionaries You Need to Know and is a Solo Change Agent with the Change Agents World Wide network and an IABC Recommended Speaker.

www.ingramcontent.com/pod-product-compliance
Lightning Source LLC
Chambersburg PA
CBHW071334210326
41597CB00015B/1454

* 9 7 8 0 6 4 8 0 8 7 9 9 1 *